Blueprints
for Awakening
Volume 1

Other books by John David
Blueprints for Awakening - Volume 2
The Great Misunderstanding
European Masters - Blueprints for Awakening
Arunachala Shiva
Papaji Amazing Grace
Arunachala Talks

Films by John David
Satori - Metamorphosis of an Awakening
The Great Misunderstanding
European Spiritual Masters - Blueprints for Awakening
Arunachala Shiva
Blueprints for Awakening - Indian Masters

Forthcoming books and films
Satsang India
Community - An Experiment in Conscious Living

Other books by Open Sky Press
Sri Ramana Maharshi — *Nan Yar (Who Am I?)*
Editions in English, German, Russian and Spanish
Papaji — *Fire of Freedom, German Edition*
Papaji — *This, German Edition*

Blueprints *for* Awakening
Volume 1

Rare dialogues with seven Indian Masters on the Teachings of Sri Ramana Maharshi.

John David

OPEN SKY PRESS
www.openskypress.com

Blueprints for Awakening
Volume I

Published by Open Sky Press Ltd.
483 Green Lanes, London N13 4BS
office@openskypress.com

All rights reserved. No part of this book may be used or reproduced in any part whatsoever without written permission. For further information please contact Open Sky Press.

First Edition
One of two volumes.

© Open Sky Press Ltd. 2015

ISBN 978-0-9574627-3-1

Cover design by Devi and Tara.
Photographs from Sri Ramana Maharshi Ashram: cover, front flap.
All other photographs from Open Sky House archive.

Printed in Poland

OPEN SKY PRESS
www.openskypress.com

Acknowledgements

I owe an enormous debt of gratitude to my two direct Masters, Osho and H.W.L. Poonja (Papaji). Without my twenty years sitting at their feet, this book could not exist. Sri Ramana Maharshi came into my life quietly and invisibly, gradually becoming my main inspiration and guide.

My gratitude also goes to all the exceptional Masters who gave their time to meet me and later to proof read their *Blueprints for Awakening* interview. Their availability to meet so many people as part of the annual Arunachala Pilgrimage Retreat gave the opportunity to collect more footage for the companion films to this book, *Blueprints for Awakening – Wisdom of the Masters*, and the series, *Blueprints for Awakening – Meeting the Master*.

An interview is a spontaneous and unique conversation. My thanks to Kali Devi for her sensitive editing of the interview transcripts, accurately produced by Aruna and Meenakshi from the original recordings. To Kali Devi, Jyoti and Amrit for their editing and patiently proofreading the manuscript over and over again!

I should like to thank Mr Sundaram, the president of Sri Ramana Ashram, for permission to use photographs of Sri Ramana Maharshi and the text from *Who Am I?* Also Kali Devi, Jyoti and Tara who have taken the majority of the photos that have not been taken from the films as stills. Swamini Pramananda, who, besides being one of the Masters interviewed for the book project, gave her expert advice on compiling the *Sanskrit* glossary. Thank you.

Thanks go to Arjuna for creating the video website, allowing so many short video extracts from the interviews to be available, to Tara and Atma for the graphic design of the numerous art pages and to Shivananda for his fine graphic advice and support with the cover design.

Thank you to Tara for her great work on *Blueprints for Awakening – Wisdom of the Masters*, the book's companion film, and the series of films of the individual Masters' interviews, *Blueprints for Awakening – Meeting the Master*. In addition, for her translation and proof reading skills and for always being ready to give aesthetic advice.

My heartfelt thanks to all the residents of the Open Sky House Communities for giving such loving, energetic support, creating a space for all those working actively on the project.

Finally my heartfelt thanks to Kali Devi, who has been a constant, reliable and invaluable support in all the stages of creating this book.

John David 2015

Bhagavan Sri
Ramana Maharshi

*I dedicate this book to
Bhagavan Sri Ramana Maharshi,
the sage of Arunachala. He came into my life
quietly, imperceptibly, through a photograph
twenty years ago, and has become a central
inspiration in my life.*

*Thank you for the exemplary life you led
and for the simplicity and clarity with which
you guide us. The question, 'Who am I?' has
provided a golden key to all who wish to know
their essential nature.*

Interview Questions

These questions are designed to unfold and explain the teachings of Bhagavan Sri Ramana Maharshi, as set out in his original booklets *Who Am I?** and *Self-Enquiry*. I believe these teachings reflect the ancient Indian wisdom.

1. Sri Ramana proposed the fundamental question, **'Who am I?'*** Who are you?

2. Many Western seekers come to India looking for enlightenment as if it is an experience. What is enlightenment?

3. Are there any qualifications for enlightenment? Is *sadhana* (spiritual practice) necessary? If yes, what form do you advise?

4. Sri Ramana said that Self-enquiry is the most direct route to realising the Self. What do you say about Self-enquiry? How to conduct Self-enquiry?

5. When Sri Ramana was asked, **'When will the realisation of the Self be gained?'** he replied, **'When the world which is what-is-seen has been removed, there will be realisation of the Self which is the seer.'** What is the true understanding of the world? How to remove the world?

6. It has been suggested that the mind must be destroyed for liberation to occur. Do you have a mind? Sri Ramana used the term *manonasa* to describe the state of liberation, meaning destroyed mind. How to destroy the mind?

7. What about *vasanas*, the tendencies of the mind? Must these be removed before Self-realisation can become permanent? Is it enough to achieve a *sattvic* (calm and peaceful) state of mind and to know one's *vasanas* so that they no longer bind? How to remove the *vasanas*?

8. At the end of his book, *Self-Enquiry*, Sri Ramana says, 'He who is thus endowed with a mind that has become subtle, and who has the experience of the Self is called a *jivanmukta*.' Is this the state that can be called Self-realised?

   He goes on, 'And when one is immersed in the ocean of bliss and has become one with it without any differentiated existence, one is called a *videhamukta*. It is the state of *videhamukti* that is referred to as the transcendent *turiya* (state). This is the final goal.' Is this the state that can be called enlightenment?

9. It appears essential to meet a *guru* and stay with that *guru*. Who is the *guru*? What is the *guru's* role? How to recognise a true *guru*?

10. Sri Ramana's devotees had tremendous devotion to him, and he to Arunachala. Please say something about *bhakti*, devotion, in the pursuit of awakening.

11. Seekers often have curious ideas about the enlightened state. Please describe your typical day and how you perceive the world.

12. You have given us a profound discourse on awakening. When you meet someone with a passion for awakening, what would your short advice be?

* Original text *Who Am I?* at the end of this book.

Contents

Introduction 1
Foreword 7

Sri Hans Raj Maharaj 15
Ajja 19
Ramesh Balsekar 43
Sri Brahmam 65
D. B. Gangolli 77
Radha Ma 101
Swami Satchidananda 127

Who Am I? 151
Glossary 163
Contact Details 173

Introduction

Blueprints for Awakening is for everyone who has an inner passion to know who they are and what they are doing here as a human being. It is for all who ask the question 'Who am I?' and for those who are looking for guidance on the teaching of Bhagavan Sri Ramana Maharshi to 'be as you are'. It covers the main issues that arise on a spiritual seeker's journey to awakening to their essential nature, to Truth. It delves into the fascinating depths of the Indian spiritual tradition, and, in that sense, it follows in the footsteps of the famous book by Paul Brunton, *A Search in Secret India*.

Twelve questions have been asked of fourteen Indian Masters who crossed my path from 2003 to 2007. I published these interviews in the form of a book and film in 2008, *Blueprints for Awakening – Indian Masters*. After the success of the first edition, I decided to bring out this revised version of the book, dividing the original for easy use into two volumes.

This book is the first volume, containing the interviews with the Masters Sri Hans Raj Maharaj, Ajja, Ramesh Balsekar, Sri Brahmam, D.B. Gangolli, Rhada Ma and Swami Satchidananda.

Volume two contains Swami Dayananda Saraswati, Ganesan, Kiran, Sri Nannagaru, Swamini Pramananda, Ma Souris and Thuli Baba.

When initiating the interviews I did not approach the Masters as a seeker but rather as a teacher wishing to clarify my own understanding and to offer a platform for each Master to give his or her blueprint to be put out into the world. A world in great need, and, hopefully, a world where these teachings will find a receptive audience. The questions are referenced to Sri Ramana Maharshi's teachings, even though the intention is for each Master to express his or her own teaching blueprint. Naturally, there is no actual blueprint as each person's spiritual journey is unique.

My own Master was Papaji, who met his Master, Sri Ramana Maharshi, in the 1940s. Sri Ramana came into my life through an original Welling portrait that I found in a pile of debris in a room I had rented in the years before I met Papaji. During my five years with Papaji he greeted a photograph of Sri Ramana every morning, and on occasion said that he spoke as a channel for him. In the last twenty years many Western *Advaita* teachers have begun teaching in the world, and Sri Ramana Maharshi is the spiritual inspiration for most of them.

During the last years of Sri Ramana's life, a small number of Westerners made it to his *ashram*, most attracted by Paul Brunton's book:

> *There are moments when I feel this power of his so greatly that I know that he has only to issue the most disturbing command and I will readily obey it. But the Maharshi is the last person in the world to place his followers in the chain of servile obedience, and allows everyone the utmost freedom of action. In this respect he is quite refreshingly different from most of the teachers and yogis I have met in India.*

Maurice Frydman, the editor of I am That, the teachings of Nisargadatta Maharaj, visited Sri Ramana in 1943. He was clearly impressed:

> *It was the immense privilege of the writer to meet a few gigantic spiritual men, but nobody ever produced on him a deeper impression than Ramana Maharshi. In him the sublime majesty of the divine life stood and moved in all simplicity. The ultimate had revealed itself as the immediate, and the undreamt had become the actual.*

The idea for this book, and particularly the films, came to me in 1993, while living in Lucknow, North India, in the *sangha* (spiritual community) of my Master, Papaji. One day I received an inner message or vision telling me to go and catch the great Indian Masters on film before they were lost to the world. I was deeply touched, but had no idea how to carry out such a task. Ten years later, after five years living in Australia, I was on my way to Europe. In between I took a personal retreat of one year in southern India, in Tiruvannamalai, at the holy mountain, Arunachala.

During my stay I made a series of interviews with David Godman, the well known editor of Sri Ramana Maharshi's teachings published as *Be As You Are*, and author of other important books on Indian *gurus*.

Introduction

The interviews were about the life, teachings and devotees of Bhagavan Sri Ramana Maharshi. These interviews were published by Open Sky Press in 2009 as *Arunachala Shiva*. During our dialogues, David insisted that Ramana's greatness came from the fact that his mind had been destroyed (*manonasa*), and that he spoke from the Self, like a wireless. While being sympathetic to this notion I had doubts about whether it was possible to be alive and have a destroyed mind. This short excerpt from David Godman in *Arunachala Shiva* sparked my curiosity and was the seed from which this book grew. My question to him was:

You say that in realisation the mind is dead, but wouldn't such a person be a zombie?
This is a misconception that many people have because they can't imagine how anyone can function, take decisions, speak, and so on, without a mind. You do all these things with your mind, or at least you think you do, so when you see a sage behaving normally in the world, you automatically assume that he too is coordinating all his activities through an entity called 'mind'. In his written works, Bhagavan uses the term manonasa *to describe the state of liberation. It means, quite unequivocally, 'destroyed mind'.*

As this notion is also believed by many of the world's seekers, such as Buddhist monks searching for no-mind, I had the idea to approach different Masters and ask them what they thought about this issue. D.B. Gangolli sums up the response of most of the Masters:
The mind cannot exist apart from the Self. It is a projection. But at the same time it is a misconception, a false appearance. So there is no question of destruction of the mind. Many people, including Ramana Maharshi, talk about this manonasa, *but it is not the correct word.* Manonigraha *can be used.* Manonigraha *means you give up the identification with the mind.*

This is supported by Swami Dayananda Saraswati:
Manonasa *is the isolation and destruction of this I that alienates you from everything else. The mind is reduced to I, and that I*

> *alienates you from everything else. When they say 'no-mind', what do they mean? They mean 'thought-free mind'. A 'thought-free mind' is an empty mind.*

And by Ramesh Balsekar:
> *Mind is something which any person requires to live in this world. What the sages mean when they say the ego has to be destroyed – but for some reason don't bother to make clear – is that doership in the ego has to be destroyed.*

With this issue as a basic question, I met the Masters for the Blueprints project. Of the Masters in this volume, several of them are already well known in the world, like Sri Hans Raj Maharaj and Ramesh Balsekar. Others are less well known, such as Sri Brahmam and Ajja, while Radha Ma would have been surprised to hear herself referred to as a Master. Swami Satchidananda was a follower of Papa Ramdas running the large Anandashram in Kerala. It is lovely to have Radha Ma in the book, with her female expression.

Several of the Masters became dear friends who graciously allowed me to introduce many people to them during my annual Arunachala Pilgrimage Retreat, which has run since 2000. Since the beginning of the project several of the Masters have left their bodies. During my retreat we visit their ashrams, where their power is still strong, and where we can connect to their energy. Additional material gathered at these later meetings has been included with the original interviews.

The basic structure of each interview uses the same twelve questions (see Interview Questions in the front of the book). However, being with an Indian Master is very different from asking a professor to explain his teaching. In each interview there was the strong energy of the Master's presence and often he or she was surrounded by a large group of devotees. In the very first interviews the questions were not yet firmly set. Later, questions were added and further questions were asked spontaneously to illuminate an answer, leading to many exceptions to the basic twelve-question structure.

Introduction

The Master's presence was always felt to add an extra, vital dimension to the interview and I searched for a way to include this presence in the book. Hence you will find a DVD Sampler in the back of this book, which contains a trailer for *Blueprints for Awakening – Wisdom of the Masters*, the companion film to volumes 1 and 2 of this book. This film includes selections from all the interviews and sets out important aspects of the teachings presented in this book. We have also created a freely available comprehensive video website, www.blueprintsforawakening.org, which offers 200 video clips of the Masters from the film, answering questions by subject. The DVD sampler also contains trailers of another four of my spiritual films.

A series of separate films, *Blueprints for Awakening – Meeting the Master*, showing each Master's complete interview as well as material filmed during subsequent visits, is available through our online shop at www.openskypress.com. A separate book and film project using material gathered from private *Satsangs* and dialogues during these visits will be published in 2016 as *Satsang India*. This project allows an even deeper meeting with the Masters.

Many of the Masters come from the ancient tradition of *Vedanta*, a metaphysical Indian philosophy derived from the *Upanishads* and from *Advaita Vedanta*. This is a non-dual school of *Vedanta* philosophy, whose chief spokesman was *Adi Shankara*, teaching the Oneness of God, soul and the universe. The exceptions to this lineage are Swami Satchidananda, who served both Papa Ramdas and Mother Krishnabai, and Ramesh Balsekar, who was with Nisargadatta Maharaj but also had a strong connection with Sri Ramana Maharshi.

All the Masters, particularly the *Vedanta* Master D.B. Gangolli, use *Sanskrit* terms. *Sanskrit*, the ancient language of *Vedic* philosophy, with its unparalleled richness of expression, has been considered the language of the gods. You will find an English explanation with each *Sanskrit* word the first time it appears in each chapter. The comprehensive glossary gives a more detailed explanation of the italicised *Sanskrit* words.

While writing this introduction, I recognise the depth of the spiritual wisdom contained in the books, the films and the video website. It is a valuable archive for those wishing to taste the Indian spiritual tradition through the grace of these Masters and I am touched that I have been able to manifest the original vision that came to me in Lucknow in 1993. It was a timely call to action as many of the Masters have since left their bodies. This archive directly concerns Indian Masters, but, as Hans Raj Maharaj says, spirituality is One. With this understanding, I sought out Western Masters and published their wisdom in a second Blueprints project in 2010, *European Masters – Blueprints for Awakening*. This is the ancient wisdom of humanity passed down through generations of Masters and their disciples.

John David 2015

Foreword

Writing about Bhagavan Sri Ramana Maharshi, or any great sage, is like celebrating the magnificent embodiment of the eternal, formless, absolute existence. They are such beautiful icons, where nature or God seems to have excelled its own excellence. When a majestic mountain range or a vast expanse of blue ocean can throw us back into ourselves without our knowledge, the great sages, with their living, their action, their speech and their every movement, can consciously take us to the same place.

One such sage in recent times was Bhagavan Sri Ramana Maharshi. As time passes, many great sages become legendary, almost to the point of becoming mythological, as the average man cannot even comprehend the possibility of the infinite wisdom they lived and loved as their own true nature. Slowly and steadily, Ramana Maharshi too shall be part of that legend, but at this moment in history he is still fresh in the minds of many as he was alive and well sixty-five years ago, to be exact! There are still some people, children in those days, to whom Bhagavan appeared as a loving grandfather figure. They enjoyed the whole atmosphere around Sri Ramana without realising the mighty presence that he was, is and shall always be!

Though attempts have been made to present Sri Ramana as a very exclusive phenomenon, everything about him showed the possibility of every person understanding the Truth that he realised as a tender teenager. He was ever ordinary, commonplace, simple and innocent, which is a natural expression of an extra-ordinary yet commonplace existence! Whether in the caves, in the solitary confinement of the temple premises, in the *ashram*, in the kitchen, interacting with the cowherds, playing with children, playing with cow Laxmi, feeding the monkeys, or discoursing with very learned and orthodox minds or secular people, he was always himself – the unhurried, the ever restful, the quiet, overwhelming presence.

That is why the memories and memoirs are full of such lovingly tender human anecdotes where Sri Ramana never made any attempt to make himself exclusive or dismissed anything frivolously. Never was there an attempt on his part to erase any part of his life or to whitewash everything as pure and sacred. He was a child from a faraway village in Tamil Nadu, growing up in a town called Madurai, exposed to the timeless traditions of *sanatana dharma* (Hinduism) in the temple celebrations and in his loving family.

Curious to know about death, the innocent youngster puts himself into physical stillness, leading ultimately to a stillness within, where everything appears to subside, yet a Presence continues without any movement at the level of thought and the body. The incident had an unforgettable impact on the innocent youngster who held and maintained it. It was only later he found the description of that state in the lives and the writings of great saints.

The immediate family, and the great tradition which talks about renunciation, vision, realisation, wisdom, the sages and the exploits of gods in all names and forms, drew the youngster to Arunachala mountain in Tiruvannamalai. As they say, the rest is history. Spending days, months and years in solitude, he found the reflections of his understanding in the writings of many sages, gloriously described in rich Tamil and *Sanskrit* literature.

Later on, with the little formal education that he had before undertaking this great pilgrimage, Sri Ramana went on to master many languages to express his vision, the Self that he was, is and shall always be. His modes of expression in different languages were shaped not only by the great Tamil saints but also by the writings of *Adi Shankara*. He was already aware of the Truth before learning to express it in any language.

In the great teaching tradition of the *Upanishads* (ancient Indian scriptures), the scriptures and teachers just 'point out' the Truth, the knowledge, the experience that every person always 'is', but is never aware of. The greatness and the blessing Bhagavan Ramana had as a youngster was to hold onto and maintain that something that everybody 'is' all the time but never gives any importance to. When somebody finds 'it', it is not even 'near' as it is one's own Self. When somebody looks for 'it', it is always far away as one is denying it as one's own Self by looking for it. One who does not look for it never finds it, either.

Foreword

Bhagavan Ramana himself would never have opened his mouth to speak, or attempted to write, had he supported the idea that no teacher, teaching, realising or thinking is needed to appreciate one's own Self. He himself was an exceptional young man to be in touch with himself accidentally, and to maintain this, but he was supremely ordinary enough to acknowledge the human need to be taught, and therefore was a compassionate teacher in his living, speaking and writing. In his day-to-day dialogue he was always hitting the bull's eye, directly moving into the 'I'. He has taken extraordinary care in his writings to deal with problems faced by the average man in the relative world. He was indeed a great blossom in the living tradition of teaching.

The beauty of the timeless tradition of the ancient wisdom, still alive in India, is that no teacher or *guru* considers himself or herself in any way exclusive. The Truth is eternal and nobody 'creates' it. Since the Truth is timeless, and therefore exiting at all times, in all places, in and through everything, it is the nature of every existing object, sentient and insentient. Hence, nobody can 'give' it to another. It is already the nature of everything and everybody.

But not many are aware of this. Everybody can grasp that they are ignorant about the world, but not many can grasp that there is ignorance about one's own Self. We question the perceptions or experiences but never question the perceiver or the experiencer. If questioning or challenging the perceptions marks the beginning of science, then challenging 'the perceiver', the 'I', marks the beginning of real thinking where the thinker himself is challenged. There are millions of people who never question their perceptions, but there are billions who never question the perceiver, the thoughts or the thinker. As a result, the vast majority of human beings live under the spell of ignorance.

This ignorance is of two kinds – ignorance about the relative, the objective world, and ignorance about the subject, the absolute. It is easier to grasp the first kind of ignorance as everybody encounters the objective world everyday. Though we 'experience' objects directly through our senses, still we do not 'know' those objects. The experience may be effortless – one may see a tree, a mountain, an ocean or a person, but unless it is named, nobody 'knows' which tree, mountain, ocean or person one experienced. The more creation is explored and named, the more aware a person becomes of his ignorance about many things.

In our generation, we feel so strongly about our ignorance of the relative world that we forget the most important, second type of ignorance: the ignorance about our own Selves. Not many of us are aware that we are ignorant about our true nature – the Self, the 'I'! Until something is 'named' we do not even know that we are ignorant about that something.

If we are asked: Do you know yourself, the 'I'? there shall be answers at various levels. I am continuously using and experiencing my sense of 'being' without a name, the nameless being, yet the name 'I' will throw anybody out of gear with a sudden awakening to ignorance, as nobody can give 'a' specific meaning to the word 'I'. The word 'I' is peculiar in that it has two levels of meaning – the relative and the absolute.

There are many answers to the question, 'Who am I?' Everybody will begin with the same word in any language. In English we begin with 'I am...' and then we fill the gap with some object or relative identity. The 'I' and the 'amness' are one and the same.

The subject 'I', the universal first name, is the same for all. But for the object, the relative identities, the second names, are just countless. I am rich, poor, young, old, Hindu, Muslim, Christian, a socialist, a monarchist. Thus, there can be thousands of relative identities. Long before we pick up any secular or religious identity, we already exist. Our sense of 'being', the existence itself, is not a matter of belief or disbelief to be picked up sometime later in life. Nor does it need the name 'I' for its existence. The existence of anything is independent of a name, and in the same way, who I am, the being, the 'I', is a nameless existence, independent of a name.

Not only is it ever existent, but also it is a continuing 'experience' as all experiences at the level of the senses, and even thoughts of all kinds, are experienced in its absolute presence. A sound, a touch, a sight, a taste or a smell is 'experienced' through corresponding sense organs to invoke sensations at the level of the body and impressions at the level of the thoughts. But 'the Experience', the Self, the awareness, is ever an experience, even before it is named as 'I'. That or this nameless being

Foreword

which is always 'the subject', and is never available for objectification, is an eternal Experience that everybody or everything 'is'!

The *Vedas* (ancient Indian *Sanskrit* texts), the *Upanishads*, the most ancient literature, the common heritage of mankind, reveal this Truth with many words, ever aware of the limitation of the words. Even though every person is always in that experience, nobody knows about that, just as we forget the planet Earth while living in our village, city, country or continent. While listening to the sound we forget our ears, while enjoying the sights we forget our ever-present eyes behind the sights, or we forget the ever-present tongue that processes the taste while enjoying various taste sensations.

Similarly, we seem to forget the ever-present Experience, the eternal awareness Existence, while losing ourselves in the sensations of various physical experiences and the feeling experiences of many thoughts and emotions. We always use our 'being', 'the Experience', long before we experience the experience of a sound, touch, taste, sight, smell, thoughts or emotions. Long before we see the word 'I' in any relative identity, we are already 'being' ourselves.

The knowledge of the Self is like the man sitting on the donkey looking for the donkey. The moment he searches for the donkey, he denies that he is the owner of the donkey. If he does not search, he does not find the donkey either. Similarly, in the search for happiness, the Self, the Infinite, the God, the Truth, one denies that one is That, and if one stops searching one does not find That either.

This is the point where the need for a *guru* comes in. The *guru* dispels the darkness or ignorance about one's own nature. The geography book does not 'create' the country or the landscape it talks about, and the *Upanishads* or the *Vedas* do not 'produce' the Truth that they reveal. The Truth, the Self, the God, does not exist because of the *Upanishads*; because That is, the book talks about it. Similarly, I am the Infinite, the Absolute, not because the *guru* says so; because I am That, the *guru* reveals it. Thus no book or *guru* becomes the authority.

But the knowledge, the *jnana*, must be freed from both doubt and error. Often we have doubt-free knowledge, but it can be erroneous. We may have no doubt that the earth is flat, but it is erroneous as the earth is round. Science begins with the doubting of perceptions. If we take for granted that the earth is flat, stationary, or the centre of the solar system, then we shall continue to remain under the spell of ignorance.

Similarly, the knowledge about one's own Self. We may have no doubt that 'I am the body', but it is erroneous as 'I' goes on shifting from 'I am the body' to 'I am the mind', 'I am the father, mother, professional', 'I am sick, healthy…' Thus this shifting 'I' is to be understood.

When the individual starts doubting the 'I' that takes so many roles, it marks the beginning of true knowledge about the Self. The *guru* takes into account the ever-changing roles and the changeless constant that is the 'I', to prove the immortality of one's 'being'. Logic is used to establish that long before the name was attributed, the nameless universe was already existing. That goes to prove that long before the universal first name, 'I', was used, the nameless being pervaded it all.

Somebody is always needed to challenge the perceptions, thoughts and individuality as most people take all these aspects for granted and never question them. When this false knowledge is given a religious sanction, in the long march of time the error is hardened as the true knowledge, and the followers become fanatical. Nobody must hide behind the infallibility of a past declaration, as that will prevent every chance of opening up to immortality from mortality, absolute peak from misery, and light of knowledge from the darkness of ignorance.

The *Upanishads* challenge the individual 'I', as that is the focal point where all identity happens. That the body is changing or ageing is natural, but 'I am changing' is an error. The teaching and the teacher facilitate the understanding of the 'I' to its true, absolute identity, and then the person learns to live and to manage with all the changes. When the knowledge of the objective world helps us to learn to use the creation more efficiently, the knowledge of the subject, the 'I', helps us to deal with all thoughts, including the 'I' thought, and the emotions, very effectively.

The Self-knowledge, the awareness of one's own true nature, does not impose any type of identity, but reveals 'the actor', the immortal, the absolute peace, who infuses every role with the touch of absolute bliss. The *guru* reveals it. A teacher or *guru* is absolutely essential. The scriptures point it out and then drop out of one's life for the person to live out his wisdom in perfect harmony with creation. It is like the driving instructor teaching driving then dropping out of one's car for the learner to drive around to his own destinations.

The relative world can ever remain a domain of constant exploration and discovery, but the absolute identity of man is known once and for all. This is '*Vedanta*', the end of all knowledge. There is nothing to know 'beyond' the Infinite, as the Infinite is all that ever 'is'! But the finite world can always be explored and the horizon of the relative knowledge shall be an ever-expanding realm!

Vedanta, the *Upanishads*, the most ancient literature, begins with the 'i', the individual, to end in 'I', the Infinite. The true teachers in the tradition reveal that Infinite to be the 'I', the individual, and to be all inclusive, where nothing or nobody stands apart. Such teachers will have no conflict with anybody or any idea whereas the ones who believe in one relative idea or identity as the Absolute shall inevitably end up in conflict. One pays a huge price by remaining sheltered, unquestioned and unchallenged in one's own unverified and unverifiable convictions.

Most of the thinkers, theologies or belief systems are busy explaining the creation or the creator, but not many begin with the 'I', the individual whose presence makes the creation and the creator a mystery. As the world shrinks with globalised communication, few can stand apart in isolation. The time has come for the world to open up, and teachers of all persuasions must be open enough to challenge and be challenged, taking into account all shades of human experiences, and never hiding behind an idea, a person, a book or anything that is beyond questioning or analysis! Absolute openness is the name of the teaching, learning and living. We can be grateful in having Bhagavan Ramana as an ever-present reminder.

Swami Suddhananda 2008

Sri Hans Raj Maharaj

You try to purify yourself by the grace of guru but you can't purify yourself; you have to take help from a guru. If you have the utmost demand for realisation you will get a guru. Until you have extreme demand for realisation you will not get a guru.

If you have extreme desire to realise, your guru will come.

Sri Hans Raj Maharaj

Sri Hans Raj Maharaj

Sacha Dham, Holy Place of Truth, was the *ashram* of Sri Hans Raj Maharaj. It is located in the tiny village of Laxman Jhulla, near Rishikesh, North India, on the banks of the rushing waters of the sacred Ganges river. It is a small and simple place, providing a home for Maharajji, his Indian disciples and their families. It's a very traditional Indian *ashram*. Maharaj left the body in October 2011.

I visited Maharaj in 2000 with a group of students from Australia. We glimpsed him over several days going to and fro to take darshan *(being in the presence of a saint) at the shrine of his master. There was a strong attraction and we were granted the rare honour of sitting with him in his room for some twenty minutes. He answered one question, briefly, and it clearly sets out his Blueprint for Awakening. We were all deeply touched by his enormous presence.*

We're living in Sydney, Australia. It's a very beautiful city, but it is very materialistic. Is there something you would like to say to the people of Sydney? Is there a message we could take to them?

I have only one message – spirituality. That is called peace. Love is not in the mind and thoughts. Love is in the heart, and that is universal. Maybe in Sydney, maybe in France, maybe in England, maybe another country – spirituality is not particular to any country.

Spirituality is the universal point. Whether it's Christ's way, Mohammed's way, Ram or Krishna's way, everybody understand one thing – love is God. Christ also said this. Mohammed also said this.

So if you want to realise God, first you have to look inside. Don't look at other people; you have so many egos inside. Do you understand?

You try to purify yourself by the grace of *guru* but you can't purify yourself; you have to take help from a *guru*. If you have the utmost demand for realisation you will get a *guru*. Until you have extreme demand for realisation you will not get a *guru*. When you get a *guru* he will open your heart. Love is open. Heart is universal to every country. You belong to Australia, another man belongs to England, another to America, another to India. But spirituality is not for a particular country or for a particular religion. Spirituality is universal and One. God is One.

For each person, *sadhana* (spiritual practice), meditation and all other things are different! Somebody sings a song, somebody does *pranayama* (breath control), somebody else does *yoga*. But the ultimate goal is One. You have to go inside, to your ego, and that ego will be removed by the grace of the *guru*, by the help of the *guru*. You can't remove that ego with your own effort. You have to search first for a *guru*. Then you will get realisation, peace, and love.

Just like dirty water that is connected with the Ganges; the Ganges automatically purifies that water. Understand? The Ganges will not come to the dirty water. The dirty water will come to the Ganges.

If you have extreme desire to realise, your *guru* will come. Your *guru* will meet you and he will give you peace. He will open your heart.

There may be a method. Maybe you go in Christ's way, a Mohammedan goes in his own way, a Hindu goes his own way. But God is One. Ultimately, the goal is One.

So, for Sydney no special message. (both laugh) As I am a spiritual man, my message is the same for every country.

John David, you explain to these people what I am telling you. You understand English. You explain all this that I am saying. If you have extreme desire to realise, you will get a *guru*.

Take this *prasad* (sweet food offered by the *guru*). Come on everybody. Immediately! (handing out *prasad* to everybody)

Ajja

Guru is the one who cannot be put into words. He is beyond any explanation. If he is a real guru he comes into your inner Self and then works on you. You can never find him, he finds you. You can find out if your subconscious mind is awakened. Then you can see the guru.

When the seer becomes one with the seen, when the seer becomes the seeing, then you lose your false identity.

Ajja

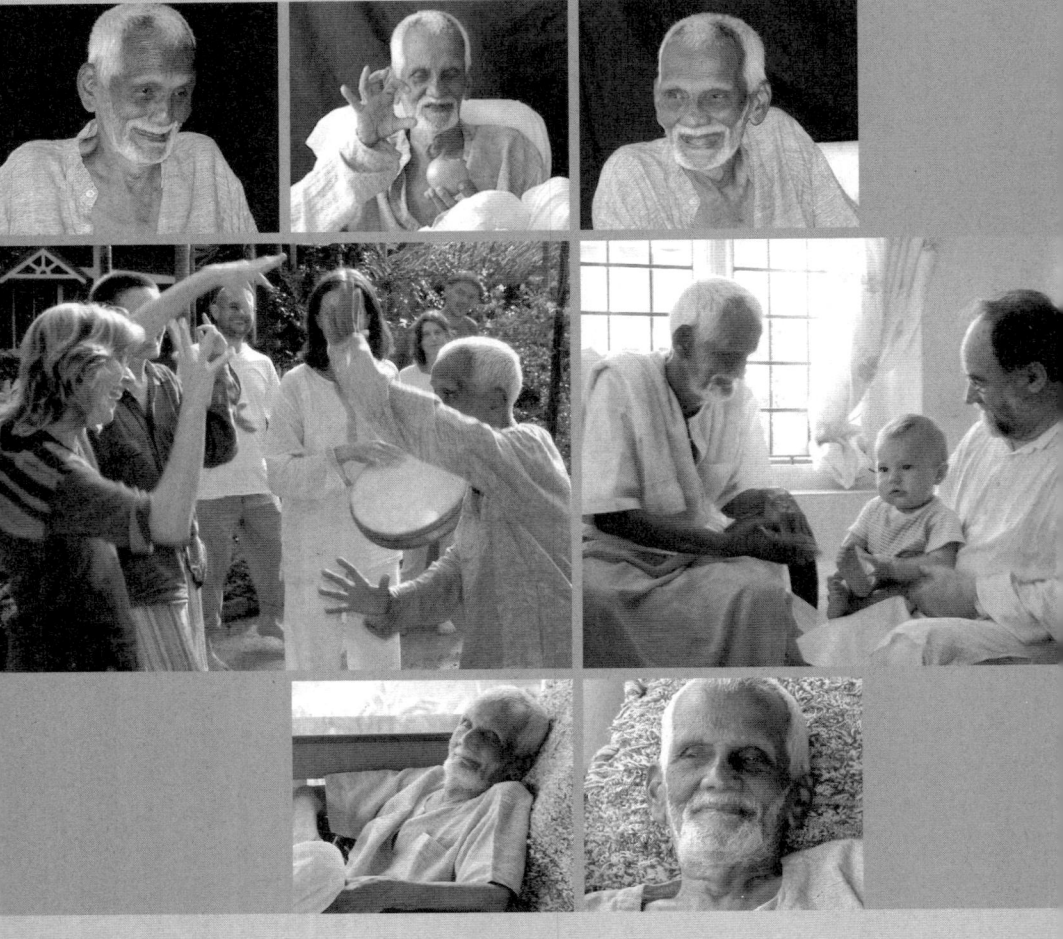

Ajja

Ajja, born Ramachandra Bhat in Nettar, India, was a modest farmer and family man until he underwent a spontaneous and dramatic awakening aged thirty-six. From that day on, he declared himself 'dead', no longer the owner of his own body. He came to Puttur, Karnataka, in 1970 and started sharing his views with like-minded persons. He lived at Ananda Kuteera in the village of Kemmai. He stuck to his famous buzzline, 'This body is not mine,' to the end. Ajja left the body on March 12th 2007, at the age of ninety-one.

Visiting Ananda Kuteera over the last five years I was always struck with the loving atmosphere amongst the residents and the playful, non-serious nature of their beloved Ajja. Over a four-year period I had the good fortune of bringing many people to meet Ajja as part of the Arunachala Pilgrimage Retreat. He always gave us a wonderful welcome, full of his wisdom and laughter. We sang, danced and made music together. All were touched by his aliveness and presence and his simply stated wisdom.

These questions are designed to unfold the ancient wisdom of India.

It's not only India, it's for universal love. It's not come only from India. So, I want to use the whole world, and beyond that also. (all laugh)

Sri Ramana proposed the fundamental question, 'Who am I?' Who are you?

Is it the fundamental question? (all laugh) Who am I? That is the second step. I want the more fundamental one, which should come from you.

I see. I think you will have to tell us.

That question, 'Who are you?' is also my question to you. If I answer that it will become a discourse. My style is not of discourse. You should ponder on it and then ask me this question. Looking at all of you people, it's as if we met earlier. So, I know you people. Do you know me?

Yes. We know you. We are all one friendship.

We are beyond that. We are not confined to the circle, we are beyond that.

We are part of the whole.

Maybe.

No separation.

That's the final stage – we are all One. The first step is we are all One; the last step is we are all One. There is something that is in between. That is 'I'. If that 'I' goes, it's the first step and the last step. Everything is. 'I', 'you'; we are all tied to this between, and if we just cross beyond that there is nothing like 'I' and 'you'. We have to go to that final stage. The first stage and the final stage are One. We have to cross the between stage.

What is that first stage? Can you grasp it? The first stage and the final stage are One, but we want to know – and we have to know – what is that first stage? The first stage is the beginning. The beginning of the *jivatman* (individual soul); beginning of the Self. The beginning of the Self is itself the end of the final stage of Self. That is Self-realisation. Formerly, in the beginning or in the initial stage, it was so pure, but in between there came impurity. Because of the impurity we say that 'I' am doing this, 'I' am doing that. Initially we were pure and after realisation we will be pure. That is all.

Are you saying this impurity is our wrong idea about 'I'?

It has already come so why do you want to think about the past or the future? Think about the present. How we view now – that is the secret.

And how is that?

If you are really pure in all ways – in talk, in work, in thinking – then it is okay. We are all here to become pure; but how to become a pure soul? That we want to know; that is the in-between. If a person is one hundred per cent pure there is nothing to worry about.

We are speaking about the present and by present I mean action – what are your present actions? How are your actions? I want to know the way you are living, your actions now.

Many Western seekers come to India looking for enlightenment as if it is an experience. What is enlightenment?

Enlightenment, in the beginning, is to know oneself; that's the first step – when you want to know about yourself, then the knower, the known and the process of knowing are the same. If all these things blend together they become One, then silence begins.

Enlightenment, Self-realisation, is a two-stage process. First is the transformation, next is evolution. First we have to transform the 'I'. The present 'I' is there and that should be transformed into 'thy': you, he – or father. Now I am the son and after a few years I will be the father, if there is a young man to be the son. The second stage, evolution, can only come after the first stage. So now you want to know about the first and the second stages.

Yes, I would like you to talk about both stages.

To whom should I say this?

You could say it to everybody who is seeking enlightenment.

It should be the heart speaking to heart. So, to whom should I say this?

To everybody. We are One heart.

You say that in presence you are One. But in presence, if I look right now, everybody is appearing differently and the bodies are all different. In the original stage it's the One, in the final stage it's the One, but in the middle part, the present part, everybody is looking different. So what do you say to this?

The bodies are different, the forms are different, but the spirit is One; the Self is One.

Do you want to speak about the spirit or beyond the spirit?

You can speak about beyond the spirit.

To go out of the spirit, first you have to speak from within the spirit. (laughs) Do you all know that you have come to this life? Have you realised that you have taken birth?

Yes. We have taken birth.

Do you believe that you are born?

The body is born, the form of the body is born, but the essential nature is never changing.

Do you mean to say that there is something different from the body? You said that the body has taken birth, so you mean to say that there is something different from the body? I want to ask a question to all of you (talks to audience): Do all of you believe that you are the body or are you something other than the body?

Audience member: I am not the body.

So you believe you are not the body. Then who are you? If you are not the body, who are you?

Audience member: I am the one who is aware of the body.

Who is that 'I' who is knowing that body? What is that 'I' referring to? The person who is not realised, says, 'I don't know anything,' but the person who has attained realisation, he also says, 'I don't have the identity so there is nothing left.' He is beyond identity; there is no identity existing.

Are there any qualifications for enlightenment? Is **sadhana** *(spiritual practice) necessary?*

It is not a question of *sadhana* but rather inquisitiveness, searching, *shodhana*. Sadhana means you are trying to see something that is not there, but searching, *shodhana*, means you search for what is there. You see the thing that is there, present. That is the finest.

If you are searching then you are seeing something in the present – you are trying to be aware of it – and there is the action that is seen, the seer, and then the object which is to be seen. When all these things blend and become One, then it becomes spirituality. That is the Oneness that you have to attain. When the seer becomes one with the seen, when the seer becomes the seeing, then you lose your false identity.

Usually in India it is said that meditation is necessary. Do you agree?

Meditation; you call it *sadhana*. What happens in meditation? In meditation the 'I' becomes the identity. The finest is searching for the known, which is there. (passing a small booklet of Ajja's teaching) You can read this, and then based on this you can ask questions.

(Reading from the booklet) 'The individual soul loses his individualised existence through right action and wisdom. He then becomes independent. He alone is liberated while alive: **jivanmukta.***'*

It says, 'Oh God, lead me from darkness towards light.'

Your questions are tricky. (all laugh)

Usually we say that we are human beings, but actually I say that it is not correct. We are in a human body. The body that you have is from your parents. But you, that 'I' which is there inside, it doesn't have any parents. That is the *omkara* (sound of universal consciousness). You are the final spirit.

Everybody should do *karma*. True *karma* (*karma yoga*) means action, and through action you transform. After *karma* comes true *jnana*, which means knowledge. Knowledge leads you to blossoming. So you have to ponder on that 'I'. You are not the body, you are the Universal Spirit; you are that *omkara*. But we do not realise this. We do not know it by experience. That is the difference. We know it through books or teachings, but we do not know it by experience. That is what we want to know again. In the initial stage, that is the real quest.

This is what we call Self-enquiry.

Self-enquiry is through the question, 'Who am I?' When we ask this question we should see the present and when the seer becomes one with the seen, then the identity loosens. If you ask the question, 'Who am I right now?' then it usually leads to this body. Right? You are going to ask the question to this body. But if you go inside and then ask the question it might lead you to somewhere else. So being an introvert is the main requirement. If you go inside, then you find *prakasha* (clarity). It is the Self-illumination; it is the *shakti* (female creative force).

Is that the final state?

No, it is the beginning. We are from the light and again becoming light. That is the process. We do not know what we were but now we are finding it. That is the path. At present in the world, when you become introverted and try to search for yourself, you always see the unreal, and then darkness and then death. This is what we are seeing now. But with transformation the false transforms into the Truth, the darkness transforms into light, and death transforms into life. Truth, light and life; all these are the basic qualities of life.

When will the realisation of the Self be gained?'

The answer to this is to understand the world; before that you need to understand yourself. So first, try to know about yourself, the 'I'. Afterwards you can think about the world.

So the answer lies in knowing oneself. How to remove the world?

Just by removing our 'bodies'. The Self is covered with 'bodies'; that is why we have lost our real identity. So first, let us dissolve from this bondage and the whole world will be anew. Not only the world. So removing the world means you have to first follow the path of *karma*, action. When the action starts, and when that transforms you, it makes you blossom. Evolve. The answer lies here.

Reading from your booklet you say: 'A man gains the bliss that is his original nature when he enquires – Who am I? What is the secret of my birth? – and engages in his duties. Upon finding out answers to these questions, his very nature then becomes bliss.' Is that right?

Yes. But before that I say all these things should be done: repeating the chanting of God's name, selfless action, believing in Truth. All these things have to be passed through. First through the path of action, secondly through the path of knowledge. Usually people start to think about knowledge only. This is a small problem.

Let's move to the next question.

When you ask a question is it for the benefit of yourself, or is it for the benefit of the whole of mankind?

For the benefit of mankind. Your eyes don't need any translation. (all laugh) (Ajja sings a song) I think now I need a translation. (all laugh)

I sang that beautiful song right now. It meant that there are not two races, there is just one race, one *dharma* (teaching of the Truth), one *atman* (individual aspect of the Self). I am for the individual and I am for the whole of mankind. But for this one race there are so many *dharmas*. Caste, colour and creed are One only. There is only one religion.

You are the beginning. You are the end. In the middle, I am here. I am giving a message for mankind, that we are One. We have to remove from our minds that we are from different religions. There is only one race, that is the human race; then there is only one religion, only one *atman*. Whatever I say is for the entire humanity. (all laugh as Ajja moves his hands)

Your hands need no translation!

If you make the enquiry 'Who am I?' The immediate answer would be 'I am this body.' But that is not what I am talking about. I am talking about the primordial 'I', the first 'I'. You have to go to that bliss which I call *nithyanandam paramanandam*. When you go to that state, the world will not be seen. This is how the world is removed.

You have to go to that supreme state of bliss. Only then is this life worthy. You are not the ones who are born out of the womb of your parents. You are Self-illuminating. The state without a state. Stateless. There is no state at all, no identity at all. That is the real bliss, the real light.

We do not belong to this world, we do not belong to this body. You said, 'When I see your eyes, Ajja, I am happy and there is no need for translation.' But who is the one who is seeing? When the seer is melted in the identity he is identity-less. So, who are you seeing? What do you mean by seeing? Who is the seer?

In these moments, there is just light.

Yes, the light is seen here. (all laugh) Just because the light is there, everything is seen; visible.

You are a bit naughty, because that's a bit tricky. (all laugh)

What's the price of your finest radio?

About 2000 rupees. (all laugh)

What is the price of this radio? (pointing to his body)

Priceless.

It is not priceless, but there is no price at all for this because an unseen power is using this body as a medium to put forth words. I am comparing this body to a radio.

Do you have a mind?

Who is the one who is questioning? Who is the one who is asking?

Now you're being tricky again.

No, it's not. This is the way it has to be.

Are you saying that these words are like a radio coming from the source? So my question is: Do you have a mind?

This is something that is beyond the mind and the intellect, which the mind and intellect cannot accept.

Can we use the word **manonasa**, *destroyed mind?*

Nobody is there to say even that, so it is left to you to decide. You have to cross beyond the barriers of the mind and the intellect. You will understand when you go beyond the mind and the intellect. You will understand that state.

Can you say something about vasanas, *the tendencies of the mind?*

(Ajja sings a song) Ajja sang a beautiful song right now. It means the answer should come; I cannot say just like that. If it comes, it comes. That's all. It has to come out naturally, then you can pick out something and then write it down. It cannot be forced.

I am asking about tendencies within the mind; these are old patterns in our psychology which repeat and they're called vasanas. *Can you say something about this?*

Please read that in the booklet. (Ajja's small teaching booklet) The mind is presently out-turned; it is extroverted. The answer is found within you. I am only a witness. I only try to bring out the answer from you. When there's a question there should be an answer also. This mere witnessing can sprout the answer within you. Where there is a question, the answer is also in you.

The 'I' which is seeing right now, it should be taken inside. The sight which is being seen, it should be taken inside. The mind is there. The sight should go inside now. Sight is seeing outside; let it find the origin.

I am giving an analogy: the sun has a lot of rays. When they are all focused at one point, at the core of the sun, there will be a big bang. When all the thoughts are focused inside, then there will be a big bang; an expansion. It's called *vikasa*, the illumination. Likewise in our heart, when all the thoughts are focused at the centre of the heart, then there will be expansion – there will be a bang.

Are you suggesting that this will be a moment of Self-realisation? Like, Aha!?

At that time there'll be no *vasanas*; when the person who feels this *vasana* is not there, the *vasana* is also not there. Then, everything is melted and all becomes One. This is real death. I am talking about the non-dual life beyond death, and death does not mean the death of the body.

The mind is travelling everywhere. We are all searching for peace; we need peace. But who is it that needs this peace? From the falseness we have to go towards the Truth. That is what is called *Satsang* (meeting in Truth). *Satsang* is the companionship of the good ones, the true ones.

I am not speaking about the death of this body, but there is some source, the energy, the root energy, which has come from the origin. So that has to be placed into the heart. At that time there will be a bang. It means a loss of identity. That is death. The death of that which is born, this energy that has come out. It is illuminating the Self. So the energy that is born has to lose its identity. Then the life starts. Which life? Life after death. That is the real life. There you can enjoy the bliss.

I agree.

The mind seeks peace.

Audience question: Please tell us how to do it?

The question was how to take the mind inwards, but the mind is already inside. So the best thing you can do is not to let it go outside. That's all. There are no steps for taking it inside. It is already inside. Just see it; be aware of it. You can do *dhyana* (meditation), with open eyes. Do the *dhyana* keeping your mind inside. Do not let it wander outside.

We can do this with Self-enquiry.

Yes, that's what I meant by Self-enquiry.

Self-enquiry is bringing us to the source.

The mind going to the heart, resting in the heart region, that is not Self-realisation. Once the mind goes and rests in the heart, subsequently what happens is *shodhana*, searching for what is really there, or *vichara*, enquiry. That would eventually lead to Self-realisation, which means losing this individuality completely.

I talk about two things. One is the path of action and the other is the path of wisdom (knowledge) or enquiry. Through the path of action the *jivatman*, the individual soul, gets transformed. Subsequently, through the path of wisdom he evolves. Evolution means he loses his individuality completely.

Audience question: Swamiji, you mentioned concentration of the mind. For example, at this moment I am feeling hunger; hunger is arising. So mind is already thinking of food – the future. It is very difficult to keep it in the present. There are obstacles. So what is the best way?

That we sleep in the waking state. During sleep the mind is visible. Let that state be in the waking state also.

Let us go and have lunch. (all laugh) That is the first step.

We are not so hungry actually. We are hungry for your wisdom, not for your food.

First, let us fill this. (patting his stomach) How to awaken? Awakening is very important. We are asleep, actually. That is why we do not know who we are. When we awake, that knowledge will come automatically, within.

On the spiritual path awakening is different from what we think it will be. First we have to try for that awakened state. What is awakening? How to awake from this sleep? If once we are awake, it is forever. Real awakening is only once. No sleep afterwards.

(Interview continues after lunch) Ajja, you have told us many wonderful things.

That you only know. I don't remember anything.

*It appears essential to met a **guru** and stay with a **guru**. Who is the **guru**?*

You are *guru* to yourself. There is no other *guru* apart from you. If you are a *guru* to yourself then you can also see a *guru* on the outside. Otherwise you can never meet a *guru*. The *guru* can be manifest or unmanifest. He can come in any form. He need not come in a physical body; it is not necessary. But it can happen only when we are in an awakened state, not in a sleep state as we are now. When we are in a sleeping state we can't know the awakened state, but in the awakened state we can know the awakened state and the sleeping state. Your daily life, your daily transactions and activities, become spiritual.

This mind can know a lot of things outside. That is science. But when you go beyond that, at the same time you can see this as well as that – both at the same time. Later on, there is no such thing as this and that. It is One. Right now, we are all different. But once we have reached there, then we can say, very rightfully, that we are One. Because we are not awakened we can only say we are all One internally, but externally we are different.

*And we need the **guru** to bring light and awaken us.*

Yes, that is what I am saying. This question is very important because each and every person should have a *guru*. We can understand and know who is a true *guru* only when we awaken. Until then we can search in different places for a *guru*.

*What is the **guru**'s role?*

If you can tell us something about the role of yourself, then we can speak about the role of the *guru*. First find out what your role is. Subsequently you will know what the role of the *guru* is.

*For example, today we are coming to you as the one who can bring the light. This is the **guru**.*

I can give that light when there is no light in you. When already it is there...

... we don't need a **guru.**

Ah, there is no need of one. What you want to know is there but it is covered with ignorance. If you just remove that ignorance you can understand and gain the knowledge of what it is and what I am. It is only because of this ignorance that you do not understand.

I need some help to take off this ignorance so I come to the **guru** *because he is a wise man.*

The *guru* is only guiding.

Dusting; taking off the dust.

Guiding towards the goal. Just removing that ignorance. When the mind is extroverted we tend to see the outer things, but when the mind is introverted then it tries to see the light. When there is no seer, when the sight itself has become one with it, then the inner Self expands and then it becomes the light. There is no such thing as seer or sight. They merge together and then there is just light. You are your own Self-*guru* and there is nothing to give light. It is already there in you. You just see.

The light is within. But there is a veil that covers this light. That is ignorance or darkness. Then this same mind, which is extroverted, is made introverted and it merges in that ignorance and veiling and explodes. What would remain is light. Once that happens, there is no one to say that there is only light – there is no individuality, there is no seer. As long as the veil is there, there is individuality. Once the veil is taken off there is no individuality; there is just light.

Does it take the help of the **guru** *to take off this dust?*

Yes, it can happen.

*The **guru** is a kind of housewife taking the dust off.*

There are many kinds of *guru*. First, the disciple should be so fine that he can find a good *guru*. Before searching for a *guru*, our mind should become introverted and find the source of the energy. That power within us leads us towards the *guru*.

*And how to tell a true **guru**?*

Guru is the one who cannot be put into words. He is beyond any explanation. If he is a real *guru* he comes into your inner Self and then works on you. You can never find him, he finds you. If your subconscious mind is awakened, then you can see the *guru*. You can find him and you can see who he is. He'll remove that dust and ignorance. Everything will be his responsibility. The *guru* will take the entire responsibility.

The *guru* works from within. With this external mind we cannot analyse the *guru*, cannot trust the *guru* at all. A *guru* can only come when the mind is introverted and the subconscious mind is awakened.

*What do you exactly mean by awakened? Because if I am really awakened I don't need a **guru** any more. The **guru** is to help me take off the dust.*

I am talking about the awakening of the subconscious mind. This is an external mind. The awakening which you are talking about is the final state. That is not what I am talking about presently. I am talking about the mind which has become introverted.

So you are saying that when I realise I am asleep and I need help to awaken, you can say then I have a kind of awakening mind that's looking for somebody to help me with my ignorance.

Yes. Once the subconscious mind is awakened, when you awaken from the sleeping state to the subconscious state, then there can be a *guru* who will come and help you, who will work on you.

So, in the moment that you are available, the guru is there.

That is the preparation that we have to do. That has to happen. You are your own *guru*, actually. To speak about a *guru* our mind should be empty, all the desires should be completed. Then you can speak about *guru*. It should be empty, totally empty. Desireless. Where do you go in search of him when all the desires completely dissolve? Then, you can feel that the *guru* is working on you.

We all fold our palms like this and pray, 'Oh God, You are in heaven.' But why do you need a God who is in heaven? He is already inside your heart; God is residing in you. Be an introvert. Let us not fight for God who is somewhere in heaven. Let us pray for one who is within ourselves, within this body itself. The one who resides in that 'I'. Let us pray to Him. We want that One. Where do we go in search of that God who is in heaven?

In oneself there is a *jivatman*, an individual soul. That *jivatman* has to be transformed, and then he becomes an *atman*, the Self-illuminating One, the light. Then you do not speak or think about all these things.

We are the creation and the Creator is there, but in this transformation we know that we are the Creator Himself. He is there inside. We are the Creator. I am the God. That transformation will take place but that is also an ignorance because God is also not permanent. He also has an identity that should cease. Who is this 'I', the new 'I', the new one who says that 'I am the God'? That is also ignorance and should cease. Only then will it be light. That is the evolution, the final state, the transformation.

Are you saying that there are two levels of awakening?

Two stages. Usually people do not understand it. (Interpreter: It is the speciality of Ajja. You can take it as you want.)

Can you explain a little bit more about these two stages?

We know we are nothing but God. That is the first stage. That is called transformation. Then we will try to say I am such a man. We will also say that I am God. I can do miracles. Usually such an ego will come when we transform. But that ego, that ignorance, should also go. That's the second stage. In that second stage the evolution takes place. For that, total meditation is the only secret. We should search and question again and again: 'Who is this I who is telling that I am God?' Only you can get the answer and remove that ignorance. It's not real transformation; it's transcending, it's the second stage.

Then there is a statement – *aham brahmasmi*. *Aham* is the feeling of 'I am the one residing in the body'. *Brahmasmi* is the feeling of 'I am God, I am *Brahma* (the Creator)'. Both these things should go. What should remain is *Brahma* only. There is no *aham*, no *asmi*, just *Brahma*. Only this, only *jyoti*, only light. There is no identity at all.

We always struggle, you know, like we have *sadhana* or spirituality, we struggle with that ego – *aham*. Or else we say we have transformed something – *aham brahmasmi* – I am the one who is residing in the body. That is like God. Both these things are distracting. So both should go and then only one should remain, that is *Brahma*. That is bliss. Only then can we be like a radio. There is nobody there. Nothing is there. Only words come, that is all.

We have been here for several hours today and you shared a lot of wisdom and understanding. When I look at your disciples I feel your heart. There is a lot of bhakti, *devotion, here. Can you say something about the role of devotion in finding Truth?*

Faith! Not the faith outside, the faith within oneself. You should feel it. Right now we are not trusting the one who is residing inside us. We are trying to find trust in the world outside but we must trust the one who is residing inside us. One has to trust oneself. We are going on searching: Who is God? But before that let us first search and understand: Who am I?

There are about ten people living in this ashram *and they give themselves to Ajja as the* guru. *But they also give themselves to the community, to the* ashram, *with selfless work and this is what I am calling* bhakti. *So my question is, how important is that giving of yourself, selflessly, in the spiritual life?*

We are doing our duties as human beings. If you want you can call it *bhakti*. If the people of this *ashram* are interested in spiritual points, Ajja is here to help them, if they are in need of food it is our duty to give them food.

My question is what is the effect of this duty for the person?

Purification. The effect is purification. Before saying anything about spirituality you have to complete your *karma*, action. You have to complete your path of work – selfless action. Unless you have done the action and the *karma* part is over, you cannot go to spirituality. So all these things which you saw are a part of completing that *karma*. The secret is to forget about what you were yesterday and from today to act with selfless motives. From today, if we undertake unselfish duties without selfish action and selfish motives, it may help us in this path towards progress.

Bhakti *is a part of everyday life in India, but in Western countries it is a little unusual. It's more rare. It seems that devotion is a very important part of the spiritual life.*

Devotion should be inward. We should be devoted to God or *guru* inwardly. Outwards means absolutely nothing. So even in the West you can do devotion. These actions are only the vehicles. Only if an action is done without the thought of 'I' can it be called a selfless action. I know how to cook, but when I cook I have some feeling, some thought. This cannot be called a selfless action. With selfless action there should be no ego there. Only those actions which are bare of the sense of 'I' and 'my' can become selfless actions.

Are you saying that **bhakti** *is a way of achieving this 'no ego' state by giving selfless service? You are, in a way, giving up this 'I' who is doing something?*

'I am giving up myself.' Even that I should not be there. It cannot be called selfless action. When we have done some good work we feel that we have done it without profit for ourselves. But even that is not selfless.

Seekers often have curious ideas about the enlightened state. Can you describe your typical day and how you perceive the world?

Whatever the answer I give, people think it is Ajja who is giving it, but it is not Ajja who is speaking. It is the Self-Illuminating One. There are no rules for me. No rules, nothing, no bounds. I am not bound by anything.

If you people, all of you, stay here right now, can anyone of us say that this place is mine? Is this yours? Is it not yours? Does this *ashram* belong to you? Does this *ashram* belong to everyone else who is present here? Anyone? This *ashram* is not mine, this *mandir* (temple) is not mine. Just like you, it does not belong to me. I am here as a witness. Your own body itself does not belong to you. When I am saying that this body is not me, not mine, then how can I say that this place is mine? How can we say, 'I am a *guru*, my *ashram*'? This thought will never arise in the mind. So there is no *guru* and no disciples and no *mandir*.

There is a difference between **guru** *and disciple because when we come here we have to wash our feet. When Ajja comes in he doesn't wash his feet. This is the difference. It's a joke. Now it's my turn to be tricky!*

You are speaking about washing the feet. I have not taken a bath for so many days. Even if I do take a bath it is by the force of somebody else. I never take a bath. If I don't take a bath I don't care. I don't care because the body is not mine. I am not the body. So the complete conviction that I'm not the body is there. So whether it is the feet or the body doesn't matter for me. I am not the body. This shirt I am wearing is not mine, this *dhoti* (lenght of cotton cloth worn around the waist) is not mine. Anybody can have this understanding.

There is a message to give: we have not taken birth for ourselves, but for the entire universe. There is a fruit in it. The fruit is not there for itself. It is there for others. It is to be distributed among all people. If you have a knowledge or a treasure, it has to be distributed.

When the *jivatman*, the individual soul, loses its individuality completely through the path of action and the path of wisdom, he becomes independent, he becomes free. He is called a *jivanmukta*. It can happen to anyone.

One who has taken birth has to die while still in this body; then he becomes free. If not, he has not really died and, if you believe in reincarnation, that soul comes back again. If it comes back it has not died. If it is really dead it cannot come back again. So the one who has come to birth, not this body, should die. Until this happens the principle of incarnation goes on until the death of that who was born. Once the real death takes places then he is liberated.

You have given us a profound discourse on awakening. When you meet someone with a passion for awakening, what would your short advice be?

Everything is in the hands of the people. Whatever you people want from me you can take. How should you take it? It depends on each individual. You can take from one who is empty in himself, empty inside. It's up to us you to pick what you want. To have the grace of God we should be free from our desires, not to let a single desire stain us. The desires are related to the mind, but what I am speaking about is beyond the mind.

Only to one who has resigned from the feelings of 'I' and 'my', only to that person, what remains is That. There is a state where action is there, but the feeling of not having done the action is also there. Action is not action, meaning though you act it is not really action. It doesn't bind. You have already come here. Since you have come here nothing is needed. You have come here with all the preparations for your return trip; you are well prepared. Is it not so?

We are very well prepared.

Similarly, why do we have to make all these problems, all these questions, all these meditations? We have been born and now it is our duty to think about how to go back. We have to go. There is no other way. Our tickets are already reserved, so we are just waiting; waiting for the right time. That waiting process is called meditation. Meditate and wait.

All of you have come here and then ask something for yourself or for the whole of mankind. But you have to go back to your place and contemplate and ponder on what I have said and then something will come out of you. That will be the right answer for you. The answer lies in contemplation and it is waiting for you.

Thank you. I am happy you have such a strong energy.

I cannot always speak like this. The energy is given by people. It depends on the people's interest.

So we will come again next year!

When you want to come next time, stay where you are, then come.

Only the bus came. We are already here, but the bus came, slowly.

Do you want the telephone number?

Definitely!

The number is One! Stay where you are, dial that number One and then you get the answer that's inside you; One.

In the Buddha's last moments he said, 'Be a light unto yourself.'

Be a *guru* to yourself, be a light unto yourself. Today's student is tomorrow's teacher. You are *guru* to yourself. You are a disciple, then you will become a *guru*. When you become a *guru* then your *guru* comes and meets you. The disciple has to turn into a *guru*, then a *guru* comes and says 'Hi'.

Sing a song or a *bhajan* (devotional song) now in your language. Whether it is French, Australian or English. Sing a song. (The interview ends in a riot of singing.)

Ramesh Balsekar

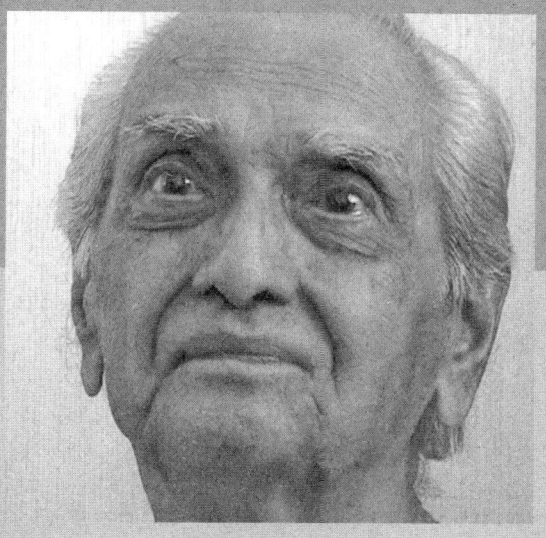

What the sages mean when they say the ego has to be destroyed – but for some reason don't bother to make clear – is that doership in the ego has to be destroyed. The ego cannot be destroyed. Similarly, the mind cannot be destroyed.

Living means, from moment to moment, never knowing whether the next moment is going to bring peace, pleasure or pain.

Ramesh Balsekar

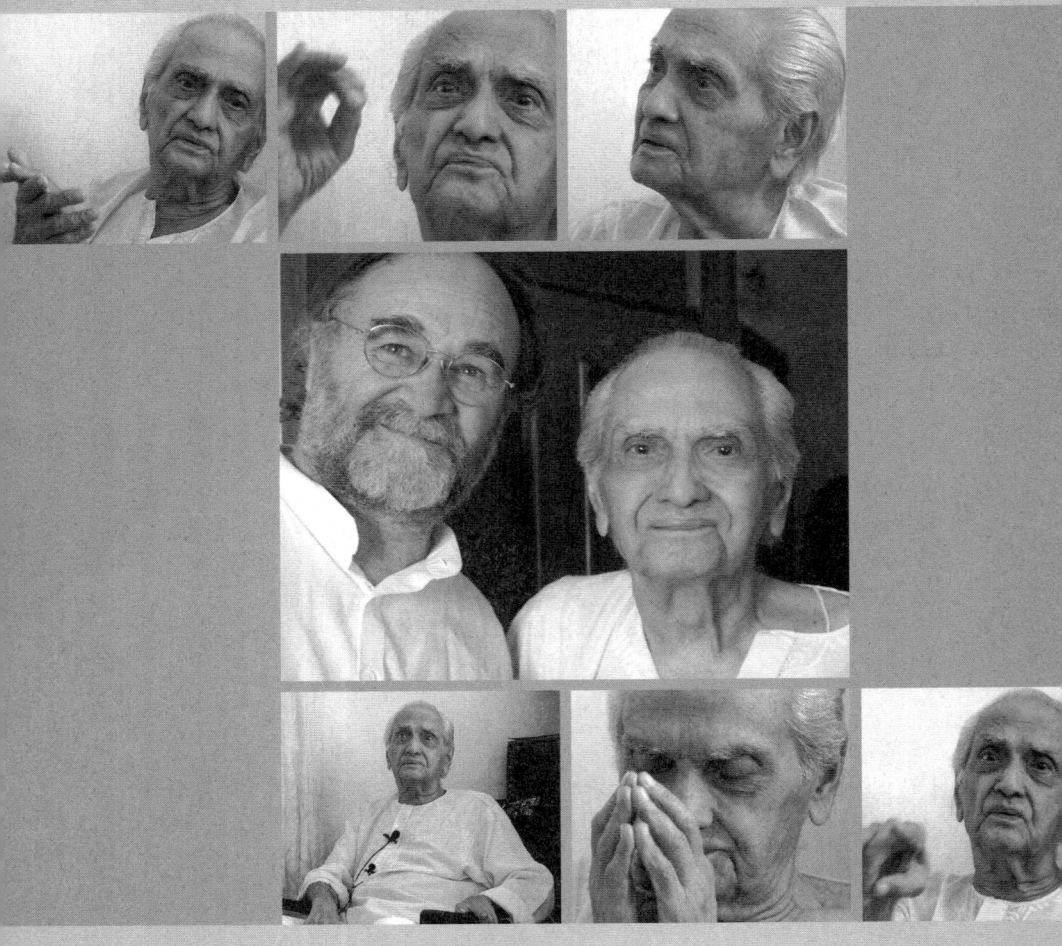

Ramesh Balsekar

Ramesh Balsekar lived his life as a householder, raising a family and having a career in the Bank of India where he rose to become president. After retirement he became Nisargadatta Maharaj's translator and later began to teach. Ramesh wrote many books on both his master's and his own teachings. Several of his disciples now teach in their own right. Ramesh left the body in 2009.

My first meeting with Ramesh was in 1992. In the following years I enjoyed sitting in his apartment, which he rarely left, while he spoke to us as non-doers, explaining that everything happens in our life according to destiny. He maintained his morning meetings for more than twenty years up to the age of ninety-two. His master was Nisargadatta Maharaj but he always displayed a deep connection to Sri Ramana Maharshi.

I have twelve questions to ask you. I've approached fourteen Indian teachers and asked each the same set of questions.

You see the extent of the madness? (both laugh) Fourteen people!

Sri Ramana proposed the fundamental question 'Who am I?' Who are you?

Are you asking me 'Who am I?'

Yes.

I would change the question to 'Who am I who thinks he is the doer of his actions as separate from the other who is a doer of his actions?' This investigation leads me to the conclusion that neither I am the doer nor the other is a doer. In fact, there is no doing, as such. All there really is is a happening of a happening. In the world, what happens is a happening according to the cosmic law. Ramana Maharshi called it Self-enquiry. I call it Self-investigation.

Are you saying that Ramesh is a manifestation of the source?

Ramesh is a name given to a three-dimensional object, which, together with billions of other three-dimensional objects, constitutes the totality of manifestation. Ramesh is a three-dimensional object from a specific species. The regular species are, according to my concept, a stone, a growing plant, an animal and a human being. In other words, the human being is an animal with senses like an animal but with the additional sense of personal doership and the dubious gift of mind-intellect that makes him tense and frustrated – but basically a three-dimensional object.

Many Western seekers come to India looking for enlightenment as if it is an experience. What is enlightenment?

Enlightenment is a happening. For a happening to happen, a three-dimensional object, a human being, is necessary, living its life as a separate entity.

So it's definitely not an experience?

Enlightenment is not an experience. An experience is what I call a free sample of what enlightenment truly means.

Like a glimpse, a **satori***?*

Yes, a glimpse.

Do many of the people that come to your **Satsang** *(meeting in Truth) have such a glimpse?*

Who has the experience depends on the person's destiny. But there is a danger in such an experience. When an experience like this happens the individual seeker may then consider himself a special person who has been offered this experience. Thereafter, instead of seeking enlightenment as he was doing before, the seeker mistakenly now seeks that experience, which to my mind is an obstruction. Whether the person gets involved in the experience or not is his destiny, but there is that danger of mistaking a sample for the real thing.

Is there a way of telling what is the real thing and what is the experience?

It is an experience, there's no question about it. The question is how much importance I give to that experience. If I have the wisdom to realise that an experience is an experience, a free sample, that is one thing, but if I consider that 'this is it! I'm enlightened!' then I go after more experiences. The real thing is there for all time.

Are there any qualifications for enlightenment? Is **sadhana** *(spiritual practice) necessary?*

Who does the *sadhana*? Someone is supposed to do the *sadhana*. So someone does the *sadhana*. Someone, some separate entity doing the *sadhana*, sees other separate entities not able to do that *sadhana*. He considers himself a special person who deserves enlightenment and to me that is a big obstruction. So if you are able to do the *sadhana* and realise that *sadhana* is just what is supposed to happen through that body-mind organism and that there is no doer of any *sadhana*, that is excellent.

Would you say that some kind of practice is a prerequisite to prepare this mind-body organism for understanding to happen?

The understanding happening is a happening. Whether that understanding happens or not is ultimately the destiny of that particular entity, according to the cosmic law. So if enlightenment is to happen, it will happen. If enlightenment is to happen without any *sadhana*, enlightenment will happen without any *sadhana*. I do not think *sadhana* is a prerequisite. In fact, that is the whole point about Ramana Maharshi; he said he was never a seeker, he didn't do any *sadhana* and the final understanding happened.

In his case it happened when he was rather young, about sixteen years old. But I guess that's a fairly rare case.

Indeed!

In the majority of cases it seems to happen more to people who spend many years in some kind of practice such as chanting or meditation.

If the final understanding is to happen without too much *sadhana*, then too much *sadhana* is not necessary, but if it is the destiny of a particular separate entity for considerable hard *sadhana* to be done, then that will happen. Nothing can happen unless it is supposed to happen according to the cosmic law and the destiny of the person concerned. That is the ultimate acceptance. There cannot be any hard and fast rule that certain things need to be done for you to get enlightenment, or that any *sadhana* will necessarily produce the result.

The ancient Indian wisdom of Vedanta *(Vedic philosophy) sets out a program for somebody who would aspire to awaken which involves many years of practice. Do you see any benefit in this ancient wisdom?*

That's an ancient practice. It is not ancient wisdom. For me, the ancient wisdom is all said in one sentence that the Buddha said twenty-five hundred years ago, ancient enough for me. 'Events happen, deeds are done, consequences happen, but there is no individual doer of any deed.' That is enlightenment.

Enlightenment is taken as a goal. It is not a goal. What do I expect to get out of enlightenment or Self-realisation for the rest of my life that I didn't have before? Why am I asking? Who is seeking enlightenment? I am. I, Ramesh, a separate entity is looking for enlightenment. So, having got enlightened, the separate entity must ask himself: What will I have for the rest of my life that I didn't have before? Unfortunately, that is the question the seeker usually doesn't go into. Enlightenment – that's what is seen as the goal.

Would you like to go into it now?

Sure. The answer has been given by the Buddha. Enlightenment means the end of suffering. Straight. No problem, no confusion. What is enlightenment? Events happen, deeds are done, consequences happen, but there is no individual doer of any deed. That is the final understanding: enlightenment. Then I have to find out what the Buddha meant by the word 'suffering'. Usually suffering would be understood as the pain in the moment. Living means, from moment to moment, never knowing whether the next moment is going to bring peace, pleasure or pain; that is life and living. What does the human being want? Pleasure all the time, no pain. So most people, when they understand that enlightenment means the end of suffering, they say, 'Yes, yes! That's what I've been looking for. No more pain in the moment, no more pain in the future, no more physical pain, no more psychological pain, no grief, no financial pain.' No more pain.

But Buddha was no fool. Buddha knew that the basis of life means living from moment to moment, never knowing whether the next moment is going to bring pain or pleasure. In fact, alternating pain and pleasure is the very basis of life and living. How can you remove it? The Buddha could not possibly have promised the end of pain in the moment. Therefore, what could the Buddha have meant by suffering? When I asked myself this question I came to the understanding that obviously enlightenment means accepting that I'm not the doer. So that ends the suffering that I have created for myself in my life because of my sense of personal doership, for me and the other. I came to the conclusion that this suffering is obvious: my carrying a load of guilt and shame for what I thought were my stupid and bad actions, and a load of hatred and malice, jealousy and envy towards the other for his actions. That is the suffering which I have been carrying because of my sense of personal doership for me and the other.

Once I'm able to accept totally that no one is a doer, that is enlightenment according to the Buddha – which I wholly accept. Then I no longer have to carry the load of guilt and suffering for my actions, hatred and malice, jealousy and envy about the other's actions. I go through life necessarily without choice, having to accept the pain or pleasure of the moment, but me, Ramesh, the ego, is always clean and pure without the impurity of guilt and shame, hatred and malice towards the other. According to me, the basis of happiness and suffering is my relationship with the other, and the ego being clean and pure in life means peace with myself and harmony with the other. For me, life means not what is happening around the universe. Life for me means what is happening in me, in my relationship with the other, whomever the other is. From morning till night there's always a relationship: at home with my wife and children, with my neighbours; when I go to the office, with my business colleagues; if I am in business, with my customers; or with a total stranger. Unless my relationship with the other is harmonious I cannot ever dream of any happiness. That is simple and clear.

So am I happy now? No. Why? Because obviously my relationship with the other is not harmonious. Why is my relationship not harmonious? Because my entire conditioning, ever since my birth, at home, in school, in society, has been that the other is a potential rival. Life means competition, life means struggle – struggle against the other. Therefore, the basis of life and living is competing with the other. With this kind of conditioning every human being has been trained to regard the other as a potential rival. How can the relationship between me and the other ever become harmonious? Only if I'm able to totally accept a revolutionary concept contrary to all previous conditioning: that if I'm not supposed to be hurt – according to my destiny, God's will or cosmic law – no power on Earth can hurt me. If it is not my destiny to be hurt and no power on Earth can hurt me, why should I regard the other as a potential danger? And if it is my destiny to be hurt, then through which body-mind organism something happens which hurts me is irrelevant, and I cannot see the whole world as a potential danger. So it is with the understanding that the other is helpless to do anything but God's will that everything is happening. How that happening affects whom is the destiny of that particular individual. I shall only be hurt if it is in my destiny to be hurt by some happening. The other is just not concerned.

If I'm able to totally accept this revolutionary concept then I have a real basis for accepting the other, but only if I'm able to accept totally that 'I' as a separate entity and the other as a separate entity are both only uniquely programmed instruments through which life happens, according to the cosmic law. Then there is no reason for me not to have a harmonious relationship with the other. We find universal brotherhood as helpless instruments. Only with this total acceptance can I get rid of the thousands of years of conditioning regarding the other as a source of potential danger.

The absolute basis of the acceptance, John David, is this: everything is a happening. Who is affected by this happening, and how, will depend on his destiny. Therefore, there is no question of my blaming and condemning anyone for any happening, neither me nor the other. Not blaming myself means not carrying a load of guilt and shame. Not blaming the other means not carrying a load of hatred and malice. Then there is harmony with the other and peace with myself. And what is left is precisely what the seeker can hope to have if enlightenment happens. That is all. In fact, I would tell the seeker this is all you're going to get; if you want something more, like the power to walk on water, you're not going to get it with this understanding; so be sure of what you want. Anything can happen in the world, but it will not be the result of this understanding, not the result of this enlightenment.

The Buddha was well known for spending many years doing very hard **sadhana.** *Now his followers are doing much* **sadhana** *in monasteries. What will Ramesh's followers be doing?*

I don't have the faintest idea, John David! I don't know who my followers are. I don't know what they'll be following.

They'll have no sadhana *to do?*

Since you mention that, let me be clear. A certain amount of *sadhana* I do recommend. The understanding that everything is a happening means acceptance of non-doership, and the acceptance of non-doership has to be total.

Would you call this surrender?

Yes, but the point I'm making is that the basic understanding is: everything is a happening; nobody does anything. Now, intellectually, who will be unable to accept it? It's easy to accept intellectually, a beautiful, lovely concept of non-doership. It relieves me from blaming myself and feeling guilty. It relieves me from blaming the other and making an enemy of them.

But for the concept to work the acceptance has to be total. What then arises is that I know it is only intellectual, I know it is not total. What do I have to do to make the intellectual acceptance total acceptance? The moment I think about it I realise the foolishness in the question. What do I have to do to be able to accept totally and be absolutely certain that I'm not the doer? Obviously nothing. There's nothing I can do, I'm not the doer! It can only happen if it's supposed to happen according to God's will, cosmic law and my destiny. Clear? It can only happen.

I accept that I have to wait until something happens, but while I'm waiting for something to happen or not to happen, is there not something I can do to pass the time? Because the doership is still there, that's the whole point. For that my answer is yes, and this is the only *sadhana* I recommend. It is very basic, it is what I call Self-investigation. I'm not asking you to drop any other *sadhana* you may be doing. If you are doing a *sadhana* you like to do, go ahead. Why should you deprive yourself of the pleasure of doing something? This is what I recommend. At the end of the day take twenty minutes off, sit quietly, be comfortable. If you like your usual glass of beer, take it. This is not a discipline. Then do some very, very simple Self-investigation. From the many activities of the day, select one action that you are certain is your action. Then do some simple investigation to find out whether it is truly your action.

The question is, 'If I consider this my action, did I decide to do this action at any time?' You will find, 'No, I didn't.' 'How did the action happen?' Then your investigation tells you, 'I happened to have a thought and that thought led to what I now call my action. If the thought had not happened then the action would not have happened; I had no control over the happening of that thought at that time and place. How can I call it my action?'

As simple as that. Then, having convinced yourself that the action which you were so sure was your action turns out not to be your action, take another action, and another. I tell you with great confidence that you may investigate any number of actions, and every single time the action which you're convinced is your action would not have happened unless something else had happened first. If I had not happened to be at a certain place and time and seen something, or heard something, or smelled something, or tasted something, or touched something, my action would not have happened and I truly had no control over the happening. Every single time, without exception, you come to the conclusion that the action which you thought was your action turns out not to be your action.

This *sadhana* makes the understanding go deeper every time you do the investigation; at some point it is more than likely that a flash of total acceptance will happen. 'I simply cannot be the doer of any action, and if I cannot be the doer of any action no one else can be the doer of an action either.' Only when this flash happens is there likely to be total removal of doubt.

Sri Ramana said that Self-enquiry is the most direct route to realising the Self. What do you say about Self-enquiry? How to conduct Self-enquiry?

I'm turning Self-enquiry into Self-investigation, and you'll find that Ramana says in plenty of places that the basis of the ego is doership. Sri Ramana Maharshi obviously knew that the ego has to be there. He knew full well that he, himself, until the moment of his death, had an ego. He called it the sage's ego, 'remnants of a burnt rope'; helpless. You can't tie the rope which is burnt; it couldn't tie anybody. Therefore, you see the sage's ego is helpless. The sage does have an ego and the ordinary person has an ego. The sage responds to his name being called, the ordinary person responds to his name being called. Where is the difference? The difference is that the ordinary person believes he is the doer and the other is a doer, whereas the sage has been able to accept totally that neither he is a doer nor the other is a doer. Therefore, in the sage's case the ego has been purified of the taint of doership. That is all.

My understanding of Self-enquiry is that Sri Ramana was suggesting that people would ask themselves who is the doer of whatever is happening. For example, 'Who is washing the dishes?' And the answer is, 'I am washing the dishes.' Then you ask, 'Who is this I?' The effect of asking this is to take attention from out there – the hands washing dishes – inside to the source. From what I understand of Self-investigation, it has exactly the same effect. Is that a correct understanding of Self-investigation?

Self-investigation is more focussed. For an ordinary person it is much easier than general Self-enquiry.

When Sri Ramana was asked, 'When will the realisation of the Self be gained?' he replied, 'When the world which is what-is-seen has been removed, there will be realisation of the Self which is the seer.' What is the true understanding of the world? How to remove the world?

The world cannot be removed. The world is there. My relationship with the other is the basis of my life in this world. When I come to the conclusion that neither I am a doer nor the other is a doer neither of us can be blamed for anything that happens in the world. The immediate result is that I don't blame anyone. I'm free of guilt and shame for myself and hatred and malice for the other. The ultimate understanding is that there has never been a creation. But we're talking about the illusory individual living his illusory life.

It has been suggested that the mind must be destroyed for liberation to occur. Do you have a mind?

Obviously I have a mind, since I'm not an idiot. My understanding is that the mind cannot be destroyed. Ramana Maharshi's understanding is the same as mine. Mind is something that any person requires to live in this world. Without the brain and the mind a person would not be able to live the rest of their life as a separate entity, yet sages talk about destroying the mind. Sages talk about destroying the ego. My point is you have to go behind what the sages say and work out what they mean. Ego cannot be destroyed, as I have explained; that is clear. We need the ego to live. Indeed, it is the ego who does the individual living.

What the sages mean when they say the ego has to be destroyed – but for some reason have not bothered to make clear – is that doership in the ego has to be destroyed. The ego cannot be destroyed. Similarly, the mind cannot be destroyed. Some aspect of the mind has to be destroyed. What aspect? Very simple: the mind has two aspects, the working mind and the thinking mind. The working mind has to be there even for a sage to live his life. For the simplest action to be done, when some planning has to be done, the working mind has to be there. In the case of a sage, the doership in the ego has been destroyed. In the mind, the thinking aspect has been destroyed, but the working mind always functions.

The working mind is always doing its job in the present moment, whereas the thinking mind is never in the present moment. The thinking mind is always either worrying and thinking about what has passed, or projecting into the future. The thinking mind creates problems, imaginary, illusory problems about what might happen, which is what causes unhappiness. In the case of a sage, he's only concerned with what happens in the moment and is not concerned with what happens in the future. Why? Because the total acceptance of 'everything is a happening' means that whatever happens in the future, no one is to blame. Therefore, the sage does not keep thinking of the future. The future has already been determined. Whatever is to happen is going to happen according to God's will, cosmic law. So it is the thinking mind aspect that is removed in the case of a sage, just as the sense of doership is removed from the ego of the sage.

My understanding is that Sri Ramana used the word manonasa.

Mano is mind, *nasha* is destruction; *manonasa*. What is to be destroyed? Not the working mind. You won't be able to live without it. Therefore, the *manonasa* is the destruction of the thinking mind.

That's very good, very clear. There is a great deal of misunderstanding about that.

Indeed!

Many of the people who sit in Buddhist monasteries for years are trying to destroy the mind.

Yes, yes.

What about vasanas, the tendencies of the mind?

Now, what is generally meant by *vasana* I refer to as conditioning. Your eyes see something, your ears hear something; promptly there is a reaction in the body-mind organism. Your eyes see something. My eyes see the same thing, but the reaction in the two bodies can be different. See what I mean? Therefore, the reaction that happens in the body-mind organism depends on what I call the programming. My concept is that we have no control over being born to particular parents, therefore we have no control over the genes in this human object. As you know, research is now bringing out the fact that more and more of what we think are our actions turn out to be a natural result of our genes.

Increasingly, research says that the genes have a greater impact than previously thought on many things that happen. You have no control over being born to particular parents, in a particular geographical environment, in a particular social status in that environment. And in that geographical and social environment you've had conditioning from day one. Conditioning at home, conditioning in society, conditioning at school, at the social level, conditioning in church or temple, continuous bombardment of conditioning. 'This is good, that is bad. You must do this. You must never do that.' It is happening continuously, and therefore my concept is that whatever you think in every moment depends on your genes, over which you have no control, and your conditioning over which you also have no control. That is why I say no action is your action. Whatever I think and do at any moment is based entirely on my genes and conditioning, which God created. Therefore, does it not simply mean that whatever I think and do at any moment is precisely what God wants me to think and do? With this understanding, I firmly believe that whatever I do is precisely what God wants me to do, therefore the consequences are also what God expects me to accept.

Vasanas are tendencies based on what? Based on, they say, your past. I say there is no past. *Vasanas* are tendencies based on my genes and my conditioning, which God created.

And must these tendencies be removed before Self-realisation can become permanent?

Vasanas cannot be removed totally. If *vasanas* could be removed then you could expect a sage to be a perfect human being. If all the *vasanas* were removed, if Self-realisation does this, you would never find a sage getting angry; no anger, no fear, only total compassion all the time. Is that how you find the sage? Nisargadatta Maharaj would become angry very quickly, and fear would also arise. When he had to go to a dentist he said, 'Will it hurt?' Fear. Anger could arise, fear could arise, compassion could arise. All these can arise in the body-mind organism over which no ego has any control.

When Sri Ramana Maharshi was asked about some of his disciples who had spent many years, maybe twenty or thirty years, sitting with him but not awakened, he said that if the vasanas *are too strong then the person won't become realised in this lifetime, and also that if somebody does become realised he can become unrealised if the* vasanas *are very strong. In other words, they can pull you out of awakening. Is that your understanding?*

No. For me realisation happens, then one cannot be pulled out of it. Realisation, ultimate understanding, cannot be unrealised. If something is a strong obstruction, realisation will not happen. Once realisation happens, there can not be unrealisation.

But I would guess that many of the people who sit regularly in your Satsang *are still very awakened one hour after, but maybe four or five hours later they're not anymore.*

Then that is their destiny, to be awake only for two hours, three hours, four hours. Basically, what happens when people listen to me is their respective destiny according God's will, cosmic law: temporary reaction or total transformation.

But isn't it their vasanas *that take them away from that after four or five hours?*

Maybe; only if that is their destiny. Their *vasanas* are removed only if they're supposed to be removed according to their destiny.

At the end of his book, Self-Enquiry, *Sri Ramana says, 'He who is thus endowed with a mind that has become subtle, and who has the experience of the Self is called a* jivanmukta.*' Is this the state that can be called Self-realised?*

Yes, sure.

He goes on, 'And when one is immersed in the ocean of bliss and has become one with it without any differentiated existence, one is called a videhamukta. *It is the state of* videhamukta *that is referred to as the transcendent* turiya *(state). This is the final goal.' Is this the state that can be called enlightenment?*

No. *Jivanmukta* is the sage who lives his life according to my concept — totally without the sense of personal doership. Also that is *videhamukta*. *Videhamukta* means free from the doership of the body. He cannot be free of the body until the last breath.

There's no question of Self-realisation and enlightenment as two different states? Shivananda, for example, talks about seven stages of enlightenment.

That's his concept.

I would like you to make it clear that there is only one understanding and that Self-realisation and enlightenment are in fact the same thing.

Self-realisation, enlightenment, means one with God. You can have half a dozen synonyms. The only question is, what do I mean by enlightenment? Enlightenment for me means the total acceptance that there is only one source, the one unmanifest source that has become the many in this phenomenal manifestation. And in the functioning of manifestation, which we call life, ego is the separate entity. Without the ego inter-human relationships wouldn't happen, and without inter-human relationships the functioning of manifestation, life as we call it, would not have happened. Therefore, the one consciousness identified itself with the many sentient objects and created separate entities, which each identified consciousness as the separate ego. Because of this, inter-human relationships happen and life happens.

It appears essential to meet a guru *and stay with that* guru. *Who is the* guru?

First and foremost there is no pure *guru*. There are many *gurus*. To which *guru* you will go depends on your destiny. Whether you go to a genuine *guru* or whether you go to a false *guru* is your destiny, and if your destiny is to go to a false *guru* for five, ten, fifteen, twenty years, you will do it. There may not be a clear distinction between false *guru* and a genuine *guru*. There may be a *guru* where the enlightenment is not total, but still teaching can happen through him.

So someone goes to a *guru* for twenty-five, thirty years. Deep down there is a frustration. There is a specific case I know. For thirty years this man was a remarkably honest and sincere *sadhaka*, spiritual seeker, but at the end of it there was a certain amount of frustration. Something made him come to me, and after two or three years he had the final understanding. Three months after he had the final understanding he was dead. He had blood cancer, leukaemia. In his own words he said, 'Ramesh, the report was practically a death sentence: galloping leukaemia. When I read it, I had never felt better in my life.' That was his destiny.

And what is the guru's *role?*

If you ask me, the *guru's* role is first to tell his disciples that whatever he says is a concept. It is not the Truth. And all that a concept can do for you is to bring you peace and harmony in life. So if the concept from the *guru* leads you to this peace and harmony, that is your destiny. The *guru* can only give his concepts. Whether the disciple will be able to accept the concepts and whether the concepts will do the disciple any good is his destiny. According to me, the duty of the *guru* is to tell the disciple it's just a concept, and also to make his own concept as clear as he possibly can so that no confusion remains in the mind of the disciple.

Is there any way a seeker can tell who is a true guru?

If the seeker knows that in the presence of a *guru* he has come home, that's his *guru*.

Sri Ramana's devotees had tremendous devotion to him and he to Arunachala. Please say something about **bhakti**, *devotion, in the pursuit of awakening.*

Whether devotion happens in a particular body-mind organism is part of his destiny, but even *bhakti* must ultimately lead to the one conclusion, according to my concept, and that is that no one is a doer. Everything happens according to the will of God or according to the cosmic law, whichever way you go.

I will tell you the story of Tukaram. He's a very famous saint from Maharastra, a total *bhakta* (devotee). He was an uneducated man who wrote more than five thousand verses. In the original story he addresses his *guru*, Vitala, the temple *Vitobha*, a representative of *Krishna* and *Vishnu*. He tells him, 'Lord, the *jnani* (one who knows) can see you as formless, but for me, please show yourself in a form which I can enjoy and pursue, which I can pray to, for Life after life.' Life after life he lived in rebirth, in devotion. See what I mean? *Bhakti*. Then when the final understanding had happened the same *bhakta*, Tukaram, goes to the temple and tells *Vitobha*, '*Vitobha*! You are a cheat! I myself didn't know that you and I are ultimately the source, but you knew and yet you extracted so many years of worship from me. You are a cheat!' The *Bhakta* suddenly becomes a *jnani*.

The *bhakta* says, *Tvameva bhakta, tvameva karta*. 'You are the doer, you are the enjoyer.' Then he says, 'You are the speaker and you are the listener. You are all there is, therefore how can the speaker be anything other than you?' Which means it may seem as if I'm speaking and John David is listening, or John David is speaking and Ramesh is listening, but the *bhakta* says it only appears like that. What is really happening is it is God functioning through both body-mind instruments, speaking through one, listening through the other. That is the difference; the *jnani* says, 'I am not the doer,' and the *bhakta* says, 'You do the speaking and you do the listening and you do the enjoying.' Basically, it's the same thing. I'm not saying that there are two different paths to reach the same goal. The words are different, but they mean the same thing. You are the only doer. You do the speaking. You begin as a *bhakta*, end as a *jnani*, or you begin as a seeking *jnani* and end as a *bhakta*.

Seekers often have curious ideas about the enlightened state. Please describe your typical day and how you perceive the world.

Now how do I live my life? The basic answer is, in any given situation, what is life? Daily, one situation after another situation. I live my life as if I have total free will, with the total understanding that I'm not the doer. Therefore, for practical purposes, I do exactly as I think I should do as if I have free will. Having done it I know that the results have never been in my control. In any given situation I decide what I want, I put in my best efforts. I do this with a total acceptance that what results has never been in my control. I don't keep thinking of the results, wishing particular things; therefore I'm not frustrated. Basically, that's what life is, isn't it? I always do what I think I should do and accept the consequences, whether they're good, bad or indifferent, as my destiny.

The last question.

Oh! Very well planned.

Yes. It must be destiny at work.

Sure.

You have given us a profound discourse on awakening. When you meet someone with a passion for awakening, what would your short advice be?

In any given situation do whatever you think you should do and never expect any result. If you keep expecting some result you'll be frustrated;

the results have never been in your control. Therefore, at any moment do whatever you think you should do as if you are the doer. Total free will. I do whatever I think I should do to get what I want, but, having done it, I forget about the results which, have never been in my control. Therefore there is no frustration. Finally, I do not condemn anyone for anything – neither myself nor the other.

Thank you.

Sri Brahmam

When you have tendencies, impressions, desires, habits, and in that moment you ask the question, 'Who am I?' it is just another thought. When we have many thoughts this question is of no use. It is only for ripe, mature people. When there is peace inside then naturally, heartfully, comes the question, 'Who am I?'

Whoever is seeking enlightenment must disappear.

Sri Brahmam

Sri Brahmam

> Sri Brahmam was born in 1944. Since childhood he always questioned the purpose of life, knowing that everybody will eventually die. When he was about six years old, a *mantra*, *Om Nama Shivaya*, arose naturally and repeated spontaneously inside him at all times. During a visit to the Sri Ramana Ashram he had a spontaneous awakening while still a young man. He worked for many years as a school teacher and in the last years, since his retirement, has made himself available to seekers.

I met Sri Brahmam through some friends whom I could see had been changed by their time with him. He could often be found in the Sri Ramana Ashram and I came to know how he had awakened within the **ashram.** *We met only once to conduct this interview. I was impressed by the clear way in which he expressed Sri Ramana's teachings.*

Sri Ramana proposed the fundamental question, 'Who am I?' Who are you?

(Silence)

When you have tendencies, impressions, desires, habits, and in that moment you ask the question, 'Who am I?' it is just another thought. When we have many thoughts this question is of no use, it is just another thought. To ask this question requires peace and purity inside. It is only for ripe, mature people. When there is peace inside then naturally, heartfully, comes the question, 'Who am I?'

If you have any impressions or desires, don't enquire, because if this question does not enter deeply into the heart it will merge into your mind and become another thought. So, first, you need peace. Peace is Self, peace is grace. Without grace, without peace, the perfect answer to the enquiry 'Who am I?' cannot arise. The answer is that all thoughts should disappear. You are questioning, 'Who am I?' If any thought arises, that is 'I'. Thought only arises with the help of 'I'. So, how can you enquire into that 'I'? Only without thoughts, otherwise the false 'I' will remain.

Here at Arunachala, by the grace of *Arunachaleswara* and Bhagavan Sri Ramana Maharshi, everyone has Self-experience. But the work cannot be completed. Why? Because there are so many tendencies, so many habits, so many activities. In these moments it is not possible to enquire, 'Who am I?' This enquiry is a deep search inside. If any thought arises, enquiry has stopped. If any light, any experience, any god, any vision arises, if you know anything, that is the false 'I' only – it is not real, and that 'I' has become one of the thoughts. You're far away from the Self. A very deep level of enquiry is necessary. There should be full consciousness. If you lose your consciousness, sleep will come, or thoughts will arise. If you lose that 'I' thought, if you don't observe it, it will produce so many thoughts. If you forget it, you go to sleep, deep sleep. Deep sleep is not helpful for realisation. Thought is a waste; sleep also is a waste.

You must be fully conscious. In consciousness there are no thoughts, no deep sleep, no sleep, no body, no world, nothing. In full consciousness, the 'I' thought merges into the Self and will disappear. Nothing to know, nothing to achieve, nothing to see. In Self-realisation, the 'I' thought disappears. Then that consciousness of Self will remain. When you reach the source of Self it is very easy to observe the rising of thought. If you observe the rising of thought very easily, then you have no problems about death, about life, about anything, because you know very clearly that the 'I' thought is an illusion. All thoughts are created by, through, this 'I'. You are always in Self, and always, when anything rises within you, you see: 'This is illusion, this is all illusion.' You don't have any problems in your life. From that experience onwards you always find the source of the 'I' thought. The Self doesn't change. But for full consciousness, awareness is needed, then there is no chance to power thoughts.

But here, again, there is the false 'I'. You already have Self-experience, you have consciousness, awareness inside. But there is the false 'I'. The Self-grace, Self-power, removes the 'I' thought. The 'I' thought will escape the awareness, and again it will arise. But this consciousness is never lost, so the 'I' thought has no power. Why? It must be born from the Self. You are the Self. How could it be born from Self? There is no chance for the 'I'. It has created so many births and now it is going to die – it cannot be still, it is trying to get strength. But there is awareness, there is grace, there is power of Self.

When the 'I' thought is going to die, automatically thoughts have no power. All your tendencies, all your habits, all your life incidents are going to die. When the false 'I' is completely dead then there is no mind, no body, no world – only Self remains. That was the case with Bhagavan Sri Ramana Maharshi. Bhagavan said, 'I am trying, I am trying so much but no thoughts.'

There was no 'I'. Bhagavan killed the 'I' permanently, with no chance for it to rise again. So, no thoughts for him, no 'I' for him. That is the enquiry. That is 'Who am I?' Observe your 'I' thought without escaping, without forgetting. Observe steadily till that thought disappears, then immediately you may reach the source of thought. But how to observe the 'I' thought? Where is it? You don't know the 'I' thought; you call it ego. Every thought is 'I', every thought is ego. How do you know: this is ego, this is the 'I' thought? When you are in meditation all thoughts disappear. You are seeing emptiness. But the emptiness is seen by the 'I' thought, and you are having an experience, 'Oh, no thoughts. I feel good. I have peace.' That experiencer is 'I'. Who is observing the emptiness? That is 'I'. So Bhagavan said, 'See the seer.' The mind is seeing from inside. From inside there is a seer; see the seer, then the problem will dissolve. There is a seer inside so there is much activity, many thoughts. If there is no seer? Then also, no thoughts; there is the feeling, 'Oh.'

Focus your keen observation directly on that seer, on that experiencer. If that experiencer falls down, your breath will stop suddenly, your mind will smash immediately. Then you are not able to control it. Then so much fear will arise, it is not easy to control. Every moment we must die. After death it is very easy to get Self-realisation because death means losing the 'I' thought. If the 'I' thought dies it is equal to death because we are dying with the 'I' thought. So, observe that 'I' thought. In emptiness there is the seer – catch him, see him and you will experience nothing inside. That is the original 'I' which remains. Focus your full strength and keen observation on that experiencer. Don't lose that keen observation. If you lose it, then thoughts will arise. So this is the process of enquiring, 'Who am I?'

When Sri Ramana was asked, 'When will the realisation of the Self be gained?' he replied, 'When the world which is what-is-seen has been removed, there will be realisation of the Self which is the seer.' What is the true understanding of the world? How to remove the world?

If you remove the 'I' thought, without thoughts, you never see the world. In deep sleep, when the 'I' thought is absent, it is not possible to see the world. Thoughts will be absent, then there is no world. It is difficult to understand because all holy persons move around in this world: 'Oh, if there is no world, how do they do their activities?' That doubt will arise in us. It is impossible for the mind to understand. Mind itself is an illusion because it is moving, it is changing, it is coming, it is going, it is absent in deep sleep. The world is seen by this mind. Mind itself is an illusion. So what about the world? It is also an illusion.

    Every Self-realised person sees only the Self. They have no illusions. They all see the same as Bhagavan: they see no difference between men and women; they don't know the world. The Self-realised person has no false 'I', he has no thoughts, he has no illusion. So there is only Self-experience. Everywhere there is the Self. Bhagavan said, 'I have no thoughts. There is only the Self everywhere. I am also the Self. I know nothing.' There is form, that is an illusion created by the false 'I'. There are attractions – are they real? They were created by the illusion of the mind. So, remove all your illusions, remove your false 'I'; then there is nothing in the world. At this superior level you are seeing the world only as Self. If you see any person, anywhere, they appear only as the Self. Real understanding of the world is possible only without the 'I' thought, the ego.

[continued on page 71]

SWAMI SATCHIDANANDA

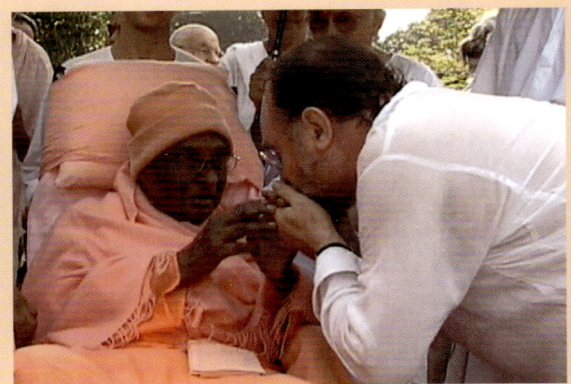

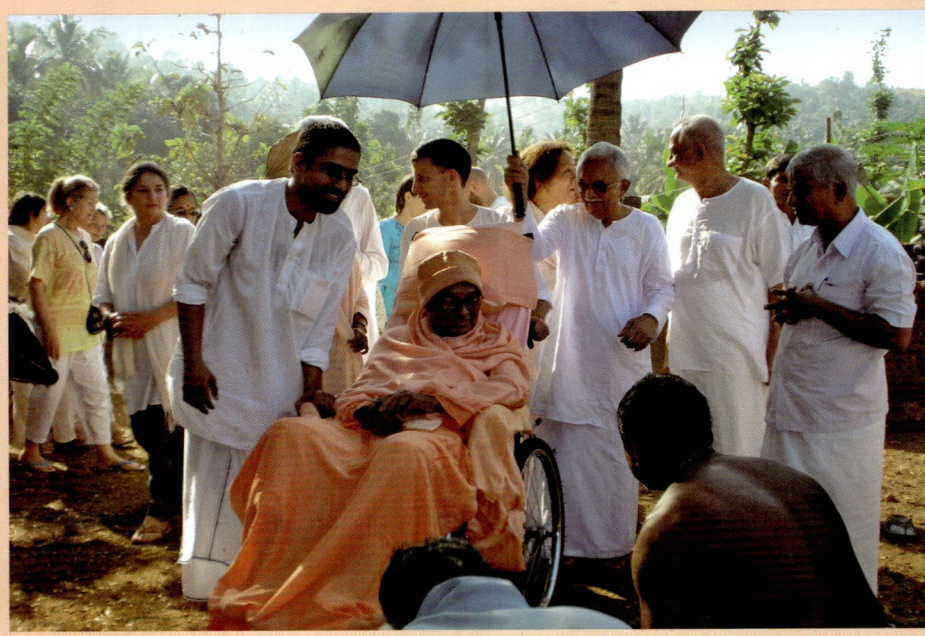

SWAMI SATCHIDANANDA

SRI HANS RAJ MAHARAJ

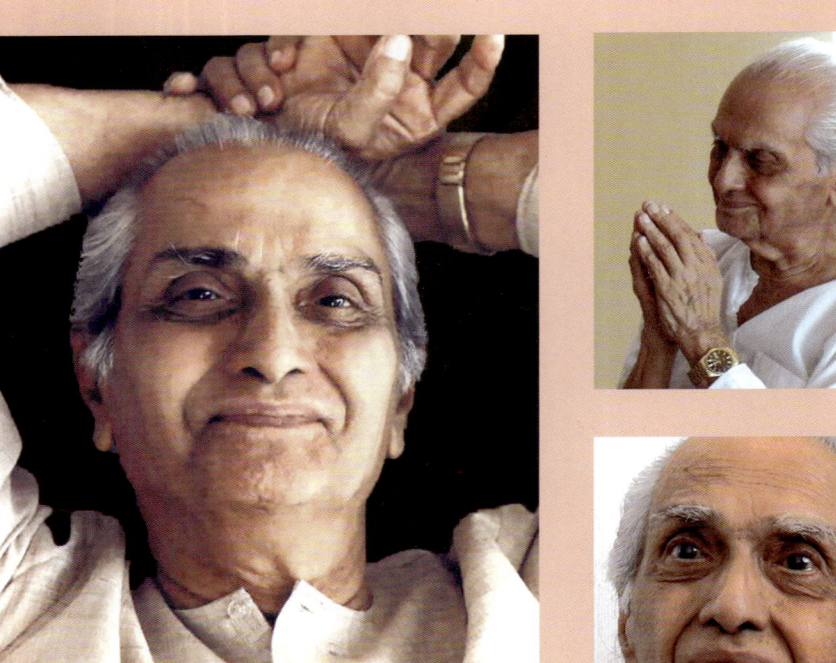

RAMESH BALSEKAR

AJJA

SRI BRAHMAM

D. B. GANGOLLI

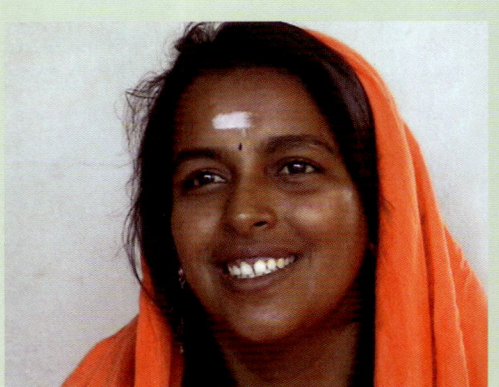

It has been suggested that the mind must be destroyed for liberation to occur. Do you have a mind? Sri Ramana used the term **manonasa** *to describe the state of liberation, meaning destroyed mind. How to destroy the mind?*

'Destroy the mind' means destroy the 'I' thought only. This is the *manonasa*. If you try to destroy the mind, thought will arise. With any effort, there is a rising of thought. So if you are trying you are creating your thoughts, and with those thoughts you are trying to remove thought. How is it possible? So, if we don't have the grace of Self we will never destroy the mind because our effort is always an illusion; our effort always creates thoughts, our effort always creates illusion. Only one who has grace has the eligibility to destroy his mind and thoughts, without effort, very naturally and very easily. If there is no 'I' thought it is not a mind, it is called the Self.

Bhagavan said, and all holy persons are saying, that surrender and trust, are necessary. If you don't trust, you are always creating illusion; the 'I' thought is creating all thoughts. I can follow the advice of a *guru* and so I say, 'I am observing my breath.' But I am creating the breath; I am creating the observer; I am creating the observer and the breath and I am seeing. Then I get peace: Oh, that peace also I am creating. I have no peace: no peace is created by me. I saw God: that God is created by me. No problem: I am creating no problem myself. What is necessary for destroying the mind? How is it possible? Where is it?

It is possible only for one who has no mind, who has no 'I' thought. This is only possible by grace, by a holy person's grace. By your effort, by your ego, too much is created. If you have any experience – 'I had an experience' – who had? Who had the experience? I had. Who is 'I'? Where is the experience in deep sleep? Where is 'I' in deep sleep? Where has 'I' gone? This is a great drama, it is called illusion. Your death, illusion; your practice, illusion; your birth, illusion. So Bhagavan said one time, 'I have no birth. You are doing *jayantis*, birth celebrations, to me – I had no birth at all.' How can you understand this? 'I see him moving and talking – why is Bhagavan saying he had no birth?' But it is true; there is no reality anywhere, within you or outside. So we must have trust, surrender.

To surrender to God one must first give up likes and dislikes. One who has like and dislikes, he never trusts, he never surrenders to God. It is true. If you have likes and dislikes, your surrender, your trust, is only drama. If you trust, you surrender immediately. To have no likes and dislikes, that is the symbol of surrender.

What about vasanas, *the tendencies of the mind? Must these be removed before Self-realisation can become permanent? Could it be enough to achieve a* sattvic *(calm and peaceful) mind?*

Before realisation you must remove *vasanas*. That is enough to achieve the peace. There is the idea that Westerners have more tendencies than Hindus or other people but this is not so. Everyone has a mind which creates. But a *sattvic* mind is needed. How do you understand calm mind? How can you tell if it is pure? Is speaking about Truth pure mind? Following service or prayer, is it pure? The Self knows, God knows the purity of us.

Gradually, day-by-day, without your effort, you will become pure. That is grace. Grace is always here, so don't think about your purity. Don't think about anything. Don't give any work to your mind. That is purity.

Give up your thinking. Don't try to understand what purity is, what meditation is. Bhagavan said, 'There is grace always within you. Keep quiet.' When you think about yourself you say, 'Oh, I am a bad fellow. I have these habits. I have this confusion. I have these *vasanas*.' If you don't think about it, you are alright. Who told you you are bad? Did God ever tell you this? No, it's the mind's creation. Stop your mind's creation only – that is enough.

All people who come here to Arunachala have eligibility for enquiry, for Self-realisation. Bhagavan said we came here because we have already done so much and here we do nothing. Grace is always within us and surrounding us. Be peaceful, joyful; all will be done perfectly, correctly. No one who came here ever failed, so trust the power that is guiding you. When grace enters us, it removes all illusion, all mind. Self-realisation becomes permanent.

Many Western seekers come to India looking for enlightenment as if it is an experience. What is enlightenment?

Whoever is seeking enlightenment must disappear. That is enlightenment. (laughter) Visions, powers, light, forms, experience – this is not enlightenment. Enlightenment means permanent peace, no death problem for you.

Such a short answer? (laughs)

Only one sentence. (all laugh) Enlightenment means the one who wants enlightenment must disappear. (all laugh)

Are there any qualifications for enlightenment?

God selects those qualifications, never us. Naturally there is a power inside us and it is removing unnecessary thoughts, unnecessary habits. Leave it to that power, that grace. The grace itself is changing us. We never change with our knowledge or effort because when we have any habits or desires we are trying to fulfil them. But grace knows what is needed and what is unnecessary, what is preventing Self-realisation – it knows. So it is always removing what is unnecessary and this brings about change. Here at Arunachala this is a natural process.

We never completely love or trust any person. Service, devotion, meditation, love, trust, surrender, are never complete. Why? There is 'I' and it cannot allow these qualities. Trust, prayer and love are also difficult. So a good method is to think about your mind, about you, and don't think about anything outside – any philosophy, any god, any lectures, anything. Always observe your mind, not the world.

If your mind is negative all the people and the whole world will appear negative. Positive thoughts create a positive world. So, good thoughts, good perception, good mind – you are good. Bad thoughts, bad perception, bad mind – you are bad. But mind is not good or bad; remove those dualities, then the mind is pure. So, observe your mind with constant awareness. Then you will realise there is no mind at that state. God is correct, your thinking is at fault; so always observe your mind. If you care about your body and your interest is on the world, you don't recognise the grace. You are wasting your time. You are wasting your life thinking about others, thinking about the world; you are wasting your valuable life. Observe your mind always, don't observe others. Don't interfere in the lives of others. Always think about yourself, 'What am I doing? What is my mind doing now?'

Sri Ramana said that Self-enquiry is the most direct route to realising the Self. What do you say about Self-enquiry?

In other methods there is a seer, seeing and seen, and all experiences are going and coming – so many methods. But in Self-inquiry the mind will be completely burnt. In other methods the 'I' thought still remains. It subsides in the Self and again it springs up. The mind has so many experiences and *vasanas* and the 'I' thought gets stronger. But in Self-enquiry, gradually the mind is burnt; it has no chance to come back. When your mind is burnt, then you get peace. In Self-enquiry, Self-realisation, there is no chance for the mind to come back. Bhagavan said it is simple, suitable, and for ever; it is permanent. Self-enquiry means being without the 'I' thought.

Is there any difference between Self-realisation and enlightenment?

If anything appears inside, that is not Self-realisation. There is nothing to see, there is no appearance. Duality is helpful for greatness, to reach divine worlds, to see gods, divine places. But Self-realisation – it is everywhere. Wherever you go, there is the Self. Bhagavan said, 'All is within you.' So the Self is everywhere.

This is possible for any person. Methods may be different but you must kill the false 'I', then there is no longer a method; that is full Self-realisation. If you don't kill the 'I' there is duality. Self-realisation and enlightenment are both the same: two different words which mean the same.

Sri Brahmam

At the end of his book, Self-Enquiry, *Sri Ramana says, 'He who is thus endowed with a mind that has become subtle, and who has the experience of the Self is called a* jivanmukta.*' Is this the state that can be called Self-realised?*

One who has realisation, who has reached beyond the mind, is a *jivanmukta*. Subtle mind means no tendencies, no attachment with the mind, no attachment with the breath, no 'I' thought.

It appears essential to meet a **guru** *and stay with that* **guru**. *Who is the* **guru**? *What is the* **guru**'s *role? How to recognise a true* **guru**?

Peace is Self. Peace is *guru*. If you sit before your *guru*, you should have peace. Then he is a true *guru*. A Self-realised person helps others attain realisation. If one has peace always within him, automatically that peace enters into others. That peace is grace, that peace is the Self.

Anyone who speaks with the mind or from memory, if he tries to learn, to know, if he is doing practice, he is not the *guru*. If he thinks any person is separate from him, he is not the *guru*. If he thinks good or bad of a person, he is not the *guru*. If he tries to understand others, he is not the *guru*.

In all states – wakening, sleep, deep sleep – he is the same and never loses his state of Self-abiding because he has no differences. That is *guru*. The Self-realised person's grace will enter directly into the Self, not into the mind. When we sit in meditation, peace, emptiness and calmness are increasing inside. Though we hear the outside sounds and there are always thoughts, there is no disturbance from them inside; that is grace, the *guru's* power. There is consciousness within you; there is full awareness within you. The *guru's* grace is going directly to the Self, Self-awareness, Self-consciousness.

Self-awareness is gradually killing your mind; it changes without your effort. Naturally grace is removing everything which is unnecessary, without your knowledge and effort. That is the grace of the *guru*. If you make any effort, it will stop. So keep quiet, be still, and the *guru's* work will be finished very soon.

With the mind it is impossible to select the perfect *guru*. You have some opinions and you see the *guru* according to your opinions. If your opinions match your ideas about a *guru* then that is the one you choose. That is a mind trick. No, this is not the correct way to choose. Peace is God, peace is grace, peace is *guru*. Bhagavan also said this. Peace is not available by our effort, by the mind; it is only possibly through the grace of the *guru* or the Self.

Seekers often have curious ideas about the enlightened state. Can you describe your typical day and how you perceive the world?

Many devotees came to Bhagavan and he advised them according to their maturity. But Bhagavan never saw anyone; he was in a thoughtless state. His personal advice is not from the mind because he sees only the Self. Divine grace flows without effort, without reason, without purpose and action. He has no world to perceive.

Is there something you would like to add?

Every person is God but they are all thinking with their mind according to their opinions. We are created by God, we are God, but through our desires and our belief that this world is real we forget our God consciousness. Remove your thoughts: 'I am the body', 'This world is real', then it is very easy to know that I am God. You are filled completely with garbage but you think it is very valuable. You are talking unnecessarily, you are living unnecessarily, you are collecting unnecessary garbage. So, day-by-day, we lose our natural state.

These thoughts are disturbing us. In the present, do good, see and speak good, then there will not be disturbances inside. There will be peace; it is very easy.

D. B. Gangolli

In deep sleep even the ego goes out of existence. Nobody will be able to say in deep sleep there is duality of any kind. It is absolute absence of duality. In other words, it is non-duality, it is pure consciousness – which can never be understood by the mind.

Naturally mind must not be destroyed. There is no question of destroying a thing which doesn't exist.

D.B. Gangolli

D. B. Gangolli

> I met Gangolli in 2003 at his simple apartment in Bangalore. He was in his mid-eighties, a little frail, a gentleman in the British mould. We dialogued about his beloved *Vedanta* for three days. In 2006 I invited him to speak at our Arunachala Pilgrimage Retreat where I experienced his joy to share *Vedanta* with a large group. He lived his life as a householder, raising a family and working as a senior sports writer for the *Times of India*. He authored many books on *Vedanta*. He left the body in 2006.

Sri Ramana proposed the fundamental question 'Who am I?' Who are you?

This is one of the most powerful and popular questions known all over the world in spiritual circles. Ramana Maharshi was a very great sage of India who hit upon a method of taking any person directly towards the ego, the 'I' notion. The *Advaita Vedanta* (non-dual teaching) of *Shankara* (religious teacher) explains, in a slightly different way, but with full force, this sort of powerful question. Many people couldn't answer that by themselves. Ramana, being a sage and a spiritual teacher also, could give certain tips on how to go about analysing this 'I' and in the process go behind the ego. Behind the ego is the pure consciousness, the *sakshi chaitanya*.

It is also called *sat-chit-ananda*. *Sat* means pure, absolute existence and *chit* means pure, absolute consciousness or knowledge and *ananda* means pure, absolute bliss. We have these three words: existence, knowledge or consciousness, and happiness. In the dual world people understand these three things in three different ways – they are not equal, not synonyms. But in *Vedanta* these three mean the same thing.

Existence means pure consciousness only, pure consciousness means pure bliss only and pure bliss means pure existence only. All the three words are borrowed from the world of duality, given some special significance and rolled into one. They mean and point to the same Absolute Reality, *Brahman*.

Ramana Maharshi, when he was asking this question, 'Who am I?' didn't give all the already known details. It is already known to everybody that 'I' is in the world, is born with a body and has some dealings in this body, in this world. There is no need to write a big book about it.

He was referring to this 'I' that is a projection of pure conciousness. He knew that this 'I' is a doorway to know, to cognise its very source that is the pure consciousness. So he adopted a method and would put this question to anybody coming to him: 'Have you concentrated your mind and tried to know who this "I" is?' And then followed a method of Self-enquiry which is given in his book, *Who Am I?*

Shankara, who came much before Ramana, was a teacher belonging to a very ancient tradition coming down from Narayana himself. In the *Bhagavad Gita* (classical Hindu scripture), *Krishna* passes the tradition to *Arjuna*, saying, 'Now I am again giving it to you.' The complete line of teachers is given in the *Bhagavad Gita*.

The ego is beautifully described by *Shankara* as *ajyasa*, which means misconception or wrong knowledge. This ego is delusory, but unfortunately it happens to be the very focal point of all empirical tasks. So naturally, what happens is many people in the world do not know how to analyse this 'I'. *Shankara* has written three pages about this misconception as an introduction to the *Brahma Sutras* and there he says it is a very peculiar combination of the reality and the false appearance. So actually it's a reality-unreality (*atman-anatman*). These have been combined together, and the child born out of the unholy marriage is this ego. Beautifully put by *Shankara*.

This ego is the effect of a combination of two things that are totally opposed. In the *jiva* (an individual embodied being) itself, the ego itself, there is a combination of the Truth and the false appearance. This ego itself is a false appearance. When this is taught by the *Vedic* scriptures, and also by *Shankara*, it is rather difficult to understand. Once you understand this it opens up everything like a master key, opens up the doors of the treasure trove of *Vedanta*. Naturally, what happens is this ego, if it is a combination of two completely opposed things, reality and unreality, will be very highly delusory. Delusion in the sense that delusion is subjective, and illusion, *maya*, the world outside in front of me, is objective.

Shankara's beautiful explanation of *maya* (illusion of the conditional world) is that a person who has this subjective delusion can always see the world because this ego has the means of cognition of the duality outside, the world. So naturally this triad is there in us – the cogniser, the means of cognition and the cognised world. The ego is to be analysed, and if you know ego very well there is no need for you to analyse the outside world for the simple reason that the outside world, in a manner of speaking, is a projection of the ego. The ego becomes a focal point on which the whole of duality hinges. So we try to analyse this ego and separate it from this triad.

Unless there is an ego there is no world because the ego is the subject that is aware of the world of duality. So naturally, if the ego turns its attention away from the world and, with the introverted mind, turns towards its very source, then it merges in its very source because it is the subtlest part of the mind. This is the very basis of *Vedanta*. Though *ajyasa*, this misconception, is the experience of everybody, the moment you cognise it as delusion it never continues to be a delusion. This is just like a spell: as long as the person is under a spell he doesn't know he is under a spell. Whatever is dictated to him by whatever is controlling his mind, he does it. But the moment he comes to know, 'I am under a delusion,' it is no longer a delusion; he is no longer under a spell.

Just as in the example of the rope appearing as a snake, the moment you come to know the reality of the rope, the falsity of the snake is spontaneous, instantaneous. There is nothing extra to be done to know the falsity of the snake. It goes out of existence. The moment you come to know the falsity of the ego, the world goes out of existence and the ego also becomes falsified, sublimated.

When Sri Ramana was asked, 'When will the realisation of the Self be gained?' he replied, 'When the world which is what-is-seen has been removed, there will be realisation of the Self which is the seer.' You have explained the true understanding of the world. You have also explained that when the ego drops, the removal of the world is instantaneous.

If the ego itself is delusory and if the world is illusory there is no question of 'getting'. Now what remains for us to do is to be rid of the delusion. As I said just now, spontaneously delusion goes out of this thing. The world is more delusory than the ego because it is far away from us and it is something outside us. Here, at least, we have got something very close to us, intensive. As long as the 'I' is there the world is there. This is a universal experience. When the 'I' is not there the world can never come into existence. We have the belief that I was born in this world. This is a belief born out of wrong knowledge (*avidya*).

It's a belief. When the scriptures tell us to analyse if the 'I' is there or not, do you think there is any duality? In other words, 'I' is the very focal point on which the whole of duality is hinging, sort of superimposed.

Perhaps we can get rid of this delusive ego, or analyse how it came into being and compare it to the Absolute Reality. In deep sleep this ego goes out of existence. Nobody will be able to say in deep sleep there is duality of any kind. It is an absolute absence of duality. In other words, it is non-duality, it is pure consciousness – which can never be understood by the mind. If Ramana had wanted to use the *Vedantic* method he could have said, 'You are asking a question about a thing which doesn't exist. Where is the question of getting rid of it?'

The moment I come to know the reality of this 'I' – from where it was projected, its very source, pure consciousness – the idea of duality was never there. It was an illusion and now it has gone. It had never had any existence at all and hence, there will be realisation of the Self, which is the seer. What Ramana means by 'seer' is pure consciousness, the witnessing consciousness. He has called it seer. I use the term witness, witnessing consciousness. You can also say, 'He is the seer.' All this duality is something seen by Him, but never outside Him. He pervades and illumines whatever is there in front of Him. That is the quality of pure consciousness.

Iswara, the Lord himself, became the *jiva*. He entered into our bodies. He created from the outside. He combined all the five elements then prepared the body. Then he saw it was inert. 'If I don't enter into it, it will never become sentient.' To make it animate and sentient he entered into it. This is a beautiful explanation of creation. Having created it, he said, 'Now I have satisfaction. I have done everything beautifully. This human being is alive and I have become this and I know everything is, and I am everything.' In that way he got satisfaction through his creation. Creation is a pretext in *Vedanta* for the scriptures and the teachers to turn our attention towards the creator, and once that purpose is served, the rescinding process starts – I am not this, I am not that (*neti-neti*).

Many Western seekers come to India looking for enlightenment as if it is an experience. What is enlightenment?

Enlightenment is a synonym for your beatitude, liberation and then Self-knowledge, your intuitive experience of the Self. All these expressions are there. Actually, enlightenment means knowledge of the Absolute Reality. Enlightenment happens to be the very core of our being and is called liberation, *moksha*.

A person who is Self-realised or who has attained Self-knowledge has intuitive knowledge of the Self, not mental or intellectual – it is intuitive knowledge. To differentiate we have used that word 'intuitive', that is pure consciousness as the Self, *sat-chit-ananda*. If this is called enlightenment it has to be experienced. It is not something to be believed in. The scriptures talk about universal experiences and comprehensive consummate experiences, *purna*, which means all-pervading. There is nothing outside this. So naturally this is an experience, which happens to be the very core of our being. All human beings can experience this. In fact, every moment of our life this experience of the witnessing consciousness is there behind the ego, supporting it, and that is why the ego is so conscious and powerful in the empirical world.

There is some conflict in this word 'experience'. I understand what you're saying, that it has to be an experience, but implicit in the word 'experience' is something that comes and goes. What you are pointing to is our very nature, so it is eternal, it doesn't come and go.

This is the empirical sort of experience. But here when we use the word 'experience' it is not in that sense. Here, at best, we can say it's a universal experience without the experiencer. Or you can also say it is the triad of the experiencer, the means of experience and the experienced object, all three rolled into one, and that is called pure consciousness.

Are there any qualifications for enlightenment?

Yes and no. If enlightenment happens to be our essential nature, where is the question of any qualification? For what? There is also no need of *sadhana* (spiritual practice). There is no spiritual practice to be done, no qualification to be had. If you look at the very core of your being, you are That. Whether you know it or not is a different matter, but you are That. 'That' means the ultimate Absolute Reality. If that is so, do we mean to say that any Tom, Dick or Harry can get this experience automatically, without doing anything? No. He is very much in this dual world as the ego, and the ego is naturally extroverted. It is always going outwards through the intellect, through the mind, the memory and the five senses, in contact with the world. The ego, the mind and the senses are called the *triputi* or the triad. This triad cannot be broken.

Any one component cannot be selected leaving the other two. See for yourself. The ego is always to be found along with these other two. If the ego becomes introverted, the other two go out of existence. The ego is directed towards the source now. So naturally the qualifications are only for the mind, which is extroverted, to be given exercises like *karma yoga* (activity as practice) and some other purifying practices that are mentioned in the *Bhagavad Gita*. There are twenty qualities to be practised positively to keep the mind introverted, and the introverted mind is directed towards its very source. This is called *mumukshatwa*, and unless a person qualifies himself as a *mumukshu*, he will not be qualified to have enlightenment.

Is that the same as a **sattvic** *(calm and peaceful) mind?*

Yes. A *sattvic* mind naturally minimises the *rajas* (active) and *tamas* (sluggish) aspects of mind but the three will always be there. Like the triad, these three *gunas* (qualities of nature) will always be there, but the person who is a *mumukshu* will try to keep a maximum of *sattva*. His mind is so very subtle, introverted and concentrated that it can think in terms of analysing all the teachings of the *Vedanta* scriptures, and naturally it can concentrate even on the Self. An introverted mind is a very concentrated and powerful faculty. So naturally those are the qualifications.

So you're saying that there is a preparation needed. What would be your advice? What kind of preparation would you suggest to achieve a quiet, introverted mind?

The *Upanishads* (ancient Indian scriptures) have given some wonderful advice. They suggest *yagna*, meaning sacrifice, and including some rituals which are conducted when you try to give up all that you possess; *dana*, meaning charity; and *tapas*, meaning austerity, where one sits in meditation for long periods, chastening or cleansing the mind. Many people are doing these *sadhanas*.

In the *Bhagavad Gita*, *karma yoga* is given as a wonderful exercise and anyone with a little discriminative power can do it without difficulty. There are four aspects of it. The first is to give up the hankering after the fruits of action. The second is to accept any work that comes and offer it as worship of God. The third is to minimise and give up attachment to and identification with the ego. Fourthly, attachment towards outside things must be minimised. If these four qualities are introduced into whatever you do it becomes a *karma yoga*, and in the course you become an introverted person and a qualified person for Self-knowledge.

After that there is what is called *sakshat sadhana*. Its three aspects must be carried out in the presence of an adept teacher. First, he explains to you the interpretations of the *Upanishads* – *shravanam*. The next step is reasoning based on those teachings – *mananam*. This is followed by reflection and intensive introspection – *nididhyasanam*. Ramana has said the same about all these direct *sadhanas*.

But these last sadhanas *that you've mentioned, aren't they going to increase rather than quieten the activity of the mind?*

No. For that very reason, perhaps, some people don't go through the *Upanishads*. In fact, all the *Upanishads* teach you about a method of superimposition, and in the process they take the mind away from the dual world and direct it towards the Self, the non-dual reality, the very source of all duality. It brings about the conviction that this is reality, not the other. That's very powerful, so naturally discrimination is very important, but in the process the mind becomes concentrated. It directs all its energies towards pure consciousness.

Sri Ramana said Self-enquiry is the most direct route to realising the Self. What do you say about Self-enquiry? How to conduct Self-enquiry?

Self-enquiry means *shravanam*, *mananam* and *nididhyasanam*, listening, reasoning and deep contemplation. When you do these under the guidance of a seasoned, adept teacher, he teaches you how to go stage-by-stage from giving up the ego, identification with the ego, to being one with the Self, which is the very essence of being.

Let me take the example of the three states of waking, dreaming and deep sleep. The teaching is to analyse the waking state in a different way than previously understood; then attention is turned towards the dream and then towards the deep sleep. First, by the way of superimposition, a relationship is built up between the three states. The waking and the dream states are seen as projections of something that is in the seed form in the deep sleep. So all three are connected. There is a cause and these are the effects. Then slowly the teacher and the *Upanishads* teach you these three are independent, not connected at all. This is also supported by universal experience. When we are in the waking state we are not in the deep sleep or dream state. When we are in the dream, waking is not there, deep sleep is not there. When we are in deep sleep, waking and dream are not there. So naturally they are independent experiences that are projected by pure consciousness, for your benefit, to know Him. All the three are projections, superimpositions on pure consciousness. If that is realised the teaching is completed.

Could you explain, in a step-by-step way, this **Vedantic** *method of Self-enquiry?*

Yes. This is capital 'S' Self-enquiry, and according to the scriptures it is actually a giving up of your identification with the small self, ego, and switching over to identification with the Self, which is your very essence of being that you can never lose. When you come to know this is real and the ego is just a false projection, a misconception, this is called Self-knowledge, Self-realisation. *Vedanta* teaches us capital 'S' Self-enquiry, and in the process it analyses everything that we have understood about the small self, the *jiva*. The *jiva* itself is the *paramatman* (supreme soul). *Paramatman* has projected itself as the *jiva*. There are not two things at all. The snake is not there independently from the rope, and in the same way the *jiva* can never exist independently from the Self, the pure consciousness.

It has been suggested that the mind must be destroyed for liberation to occur. Do you have a mind? Sri Ramana used the term **manonasa** *to describe the state of liberation, meaning destroyed mind. How to destroy the mind?*

'It has been suggested that the mind must be destroyed…' You see, mind, at present, appears to be there. Mind means ego; the subtlest aspect of the mind is ego and the intellect is there. The memory aspect of it is also there. So mind means all these four aspects – the ego, the intellect, the memory aspect, and the volitionary – all these comprise the mind.

Now we in the empirical sphere, we accept that the mind exists, don't we? But when we come to know the reality of the Self, mind is not there at all. It was never there. So naturally the mind need not be destroyed – there is no question of destroying a thing that doesn't exist. World can exist only when the ego is there. Without the ego the world can never be experienced, can never exist. It's the same here, the mind cannot exist apart from the Self. It is a projection. But, at the same time, it is a misconception, a false appearance. So there is no question of destruction of the mind. Many people, including Ramana Maharshi, talk about this *manonasa*, destruction of the mind, but it is not the correct word. *Manonigra* can be used. *Manonigra* means you give up the identification with the mind, give up grasping anything, and when there is no grasping, the grasper also is not there.

What about vasanas, *the tendencies of the mind? Must these be removed before Self-realisation can become permanent?*

Vasanas are latent impressions. These latent impressions are taught in a beautiful manner. You know, it's a vicious circle. As long as you have got *avidya*, ignorance of the Self, the ego will be there. *Avidya* itself is *ajyasa*, misconception, so the ego will be there. Can you find an ego without any desires? Never. An ego without desires can never be found.

If you analyse the ego properly, according to the *Vedantic* scriptures, it is a bundle of desires, and when these desires become very powerful they prompt you into action because the desire is towards acquiring something from the outside world. So we are prompted to take action – go there, procure it, secure it and then take it in our possession. So desire leads to *karma*, action. *Karma* leads to *karmaphala*, the result of an action. Any action has to reap its fruit, and whether it is good or bad, you, the agent of the action, has to enjoy it. When you enjoy the fruit, there is a latent impression created in the mind and that's called the *vasana*. The *vasana* is lurking even in the unconscious mind, where it becomes very powerful. When favourable conditions are created here in the world, those latent impressions come to the surface in the form of powerful desires that prompt us again into action.

So this is how, like the dog trying to catch its tail, we are going through the vicious circle of repeated births and deaths. This is called *samsara*. But this can be removed very easily with Self-knowledge. The moment the ignorance of the Self goes out of existence, there is no *samsara*. You have gotten rid of the *samsara* and all the problems of life.

Self-realisation means getting rid of all these false appearances. You must never give that same stamp of reality as you give to the Self to anything from the ego or the mind.

During the time I spent with my master, Poonjaji, there were people, who, in his presence, had a very strong awakening to the Self, and he would say, 'Your work is finished.' They would be glowing in bliss and they would feel their work was finished. Then they would go away for some months and when they came back a lot of these people would say, 'It's gone!' Often Poonjaji would say, 'If it's gone, then you never found it in the beginning.' And at the same time, I can remember Sri Ramana saying that strong vasanas can pull you out of that awakening, that understanding. Can you comment on that?

There are many people who speak in terms of *shaktipatta*. Have you heard of it?

Yes, it's a kind of transmission of energy.

Vedanta never approves of that. These things cannot be transferred from one person to another. If you speak in terms of transfer at all, it is the *guru* telling you to find it in yourself. There is no transfer, so this *shaktipatta* is a misnomer and is totally wrong. It is never taught in the *Upanishads* and I don't know how Poonjaji and all these people got this understanding. *Vedanta* doesn't approve of any mysticism. There are many mystics.

I didn't experience Poonjaji as a mystic. He would simply sit there and people would come and ask him questions.

Self-knowledge doesn't need any certificate from any mystic. The *Upanishads* are supposed to be of divine origin. The *rishis* (seers) became the medium through which the *Upanishads* were heard and articulated and given to the world. It is divinity itself that is called the *Upanishad purusha*, the Self. It is to be known only through the *Upanishads*, nothing else. So, if this is what *Shankara* teaches us, and what *Vedanta* teaches, then the mystics cannot be trusted. There is no such thing as an experience that can be taught in terms of universal experiences.

I understand what you are saying in one way, but surely if the seeker is ripe and he comes to a master who turns the thing back around to the student with a certain force in that moment, then surely it is possible that that is the moment when the student finally sees the Truth and there is no magic in it.

I don't agree with that because it is there in him. Nothing is given to him afresh by the *guru*.

No, nothing is given, but just by the **guru**'s *presence there is an end, there is a finality.*

Alright, in that case, the moment I know the Self I have gained Self-knowledge. I don't see anything, no world at all. I don't hear *om* (sound of universal consciousness) and see brilliant light everywhere; nothing of the kind. If that were so, *Shankara* would have mentioned it somewhere. The *Upanishads* would have mentioned it.

In the Japanese Zen tradition there is a whole history of stories where, at a certain moment, the master touches the student in some way and the student wakes up. This is similar to what I am describing.

Anything that is created afresh is created in time and it will go out of existence. But Self-knowledge is not of that kind. It is beyond time, space and causation. It is neither a cause nor an effect.

I don't think these people experienced any transfer of energy from Poonjaji to themselves, but more they experienced the end of the search. Perhaps they were mature people who had been looking for understanding in many places, for many years, and in this particular man's presence they were taken back or forced into the deep recess inside themselves and then experienced the Self.

I can accept that, in a qualified manner. Let us put it this way: the adept teacher invokes, kindles, that Self-knowledge in the student. But when the Self-knowledge is attained, he realises. That is called Self-realisation, isn't it? When he realises that Self, should there be any sort of superhuman symptom or symbol that is occurring in him?

If realisation has happened, the student will attain *sirvatmabhava* – everything is nothing but *atman*, the Self. Ramana had that understanding; we can't doubt it. This was the reason for his blank expression. He was completely identified with the Self. That is where he was looking from, and he had separated the Self from the not-Self. Unless you do that you can't have that blank look. He was identified with the Self in every moment. He was not registering any experience.

I would like to tell you my own experience with Poonjaji. After more than twenty years of searching, doing sadhana *and so on, I was suddenly sitting in front of this man who had a tremendous energy and was the focus of two hundred people. He talked to me personally in a way that seemed to turn all the energy back inside me. I didn't feel any transmission from him, but something occurred inside me. There was whiteness, nothingness. Suddenly I discovered I couldn't open my eyes. They physically wouldn't open. I was transfixed in that place. At the end of all this, when I had been given some water and was just resting, there was tremendous bliss. There was no John David, there was no mind. There was a tremendous expansion of consciousness.*

In *Vedanta*, we dismiss these individualistic things; they are not universal experiences. *Upasanas* are meditations that are mentioned in the scriptures. You perform them as they are given to you, to the letter, very carefully. You get such mystic powers and each one gives rise to a different kind of experience. It's an experience, it is individualistic, but we are not talking about that. It is a sign that you are on the right way. It is a certificate that you are getting your mind clarified, but these meditations can never give you the ultimate. You have to come to *jnana* (knowledge, wisdom) only, which is an intuitive experience of the Self and is based on universal experiences like waking, dream and deep sleep. Deep sleep is an experience that is experienced by everybody, and, in deep sleep, pure consciousness is in its purest form, not having any superimposition nor any projection. There is no white light, nothing of the kind. That is taught by the *Upanishads*. Why not accept it? It is based on universal experiences. You can never deny that.

But why would I deny my own personal experience?

You see, the point is many people have followed Poonjaji and others. They have had all sorts of brilliant experiences. First and foremost, Self-realisation is a thing that is not to be got afresh. Secondly, it happens to be the very core of our being, whether we know it or not. There's no choice for it and hence, in that light, it is destined. You are destined to be one with it. From that point of view you can call it destiny. You are destined to be That only.

From one day to the next all the questions went and I saw that the ground of being was always there, the Self. From that moment it seemed as if I was thrust deeply into the ocean of Self, which I have never left.

A Self-realised person expressing the same thing would say: 'The moment I get *jnana*, my identification with the ego is minimised. I don't seek anything. There's nothing, no purpose in having anything.' He speaks the language of a renunciate. He has renounced everything, all of duality; he doesn't possess even the body now. The greatest fear one can have is the fear of death. He has already gone beyond death, so he is not afraid of it. He can say, 'Death, you can come and take away this body. I have already discarded it.'

That's also my situation.

Actually, many people have got it, but they didn't have this special thing that you had. The understanding is more important than the light and other experiences.

I should be clear. I never considered that actual experience of light and expansion, in itself, to be important. The thing that seemed to be important was the entrance into the ground of being, which has never left.

Yes, that is more important.

It has never left.

Yes, it will never leave. It never came and it never left. It was always there.

This was always there. The duality, and other things which I believed to be true, they were never there – well, they seemed to be there.

They seemed to be there, but they were never there.

Right, but the thing that changed in that moment was a clear knowing of the ground of being. In that moment, it changed everything in such a way that there were no more questions. The knowing hadn't been there before, but has been there ever since.

Yes, correct. Knowing the Self is not the usual knowing by the intellect. That's not knowing – you can never know the Self that way, as an object. It can never become the object. The Self, pure consciousness, at best can become the subject in the form of the ego, which goes to show the concessions that the *Upanishads* give to us. It is the pure consciousness, the Self, coming in the form of the ego. Beyond that, it can never become an object, but, at best, it can become a subject that is conscious of the object. That's all; it can never be made the object. So naturally 'I' itself, in its own realm, can never be objectified by anything else. The only thing that can objectify the ego is the pure consciousness. But in the sphere of duality, ego can never be objectified. It is the subject; it will remain like that. For that very reason 'I' can never give up the ego, the subjective consciousness in me; 'I' can never jump out of it and become the object. 'I' can always remain the source of awareness in the duality sphere. I know everything else, but that ego, such a powerful ego, even though it is in the presence of the Self, it is sort of a misconception. It never really existed apart from the Self.

The Self itself appears as the ego, and when the ego seeks its source, that is called Self-realisation. That's all. And Self-realisation doesn't mean Self is objectified, experienced. Nothing like that. You remain as the Self. Are you aware of the Self, the ego? Supposing we put that question to ourselves: Are we aware of the ego? What will the answer be? In the sphere of duality, ego is the basic focal point on which all duality is mounted, or superimposed. Now ego itself, is it self-aware? Yes! It is self-established and it can never give up its self-awareness. Very true. In the world of duality, Self can never be objectified by anything else. Hence, it has the stamp of certainty, even though it is a misconception. Wonderful! This is something fantastic. The ego itself, in the sphere of duality, has the stamp of reality. It doesn't need any certificate of being real, yet from the viewpoint of the pure consciousness, it was a misconception of Truth which was superimposed.

So, it is the Self trying to show its excellences – it can project the world through the ego and again take it back. This is His *leela*, His divine play. The play of the Self, of *paramatman*, God. He is doing this in every moment. Should He create the world? Is it true? It is given in the form of a story, but it is not true that way. These are all pretexts for the teacher and the scriptures to turn our attention towards the Absolute Reality. That's all. Nothing else.

At the end of his book, **Self-Enquiry,** *Sri Ramana says, 'He who is thus endowed with a mind that has become subtle and who has the experience of the Self is called a* **jivanmukta.***'*

This kind of subtle mind has become One with the ultimate Reality. The *Vedanta* scriptures say that spiritual instruction given by a teacher who knows the tradition can result in some sort of a refinement in the mind, which happened in your case in front of Poonjaji. Ultimately, when the mind becomes refined by these teachings it becomes no-mind. It merges in its very source. So a *jivanmukta* can be interpreted as a person who has established himself in this pure consciousness. Although he is still in the body, he feels he is no more embodied – as if he is one with the Self, not with this self. This self has been sublimated, falsified, and even if he carries out any transactions through this ego he fully knows that he is acting. The *jivanmukta* is acting as an actor, wearing the role of this small self. Ego and he know, 'I have nothing to gain here. I have to keep this body going as long as it can because it has taken a shape, and let it go on as long as it lives. Let it live.' In the *Bhagavad Gita*, Krishna says to *Arjuna*, 'Don't harm this body because this vehicle helped you to come to this stage. It has helped you. It has become a medium for you to achieve this wisdom and so many other arts.' He didn't say, 'Now your job is done so throw it out.' Don't do that. Let it fall off of its own accord.

Sri Ramana goes on, 'And when one is immersed in the ocean of bliss and has become one with it without any differentiated existence, one is called a videhamukta.'

Videhamukta means without the body. You see, *mukta* means with the body, *jivanmukta*. *Videhamukta* means that after giving up the body he becomes One with the Ultimate. This is a thing which is not accepted by *Vedanta* and if it was said by Ramana, he is going against the *Upanishads*. *Videha* (without the body) is not taught at all by the *Upanishads*. This was introduced by the people who came much later than *Shankara*. *Jivanmukta* occurs at any time while in the body. The body may continue but you are not identified with the body. You have identified with the Self and you have separated the not-self, the body, and the reality of the consciousness. So you are established in the reality. A *jivanmukta*, while in the body, has known the essential nature of liberation, freedom, and that is called the Self.

It appears essential to meet a guru *and stay with that* guru. *Who is the* guru?

The *Mundika Upanishad* – *mundika* means shaven head, so it signifies it is meant for the *sannyasins*, the renunciates – says you must find the *guru* who is a *shrutriya* and a *brahmanishta*. *Shrutriya* means he must be very well versed in the traditional method of teaching, and *brahmanishta* means he must be established in the ultimate Reality. So these are the qualifications of a *guru*.

And what is the guru's *role?*

The *guru's* role is only to teach the methods for giving up identification with the ego, the embodied self, and realising one's essential nature. That is his role. He has studied the scriptures, the methods; he has been taught by his *guru*, so he was also at one time a student. Then he remembers all the impediments, the difficulties he experienced as a student and how he got rid of all his doubts. Now he is in the position of the *guru*, and he teaches the student according to that method. The student also will become a light kindling another light; so this goes on in a series. That is the *guru's* role.

And how to recognise a true guru?

When you come in close contact with the *guru*, you see how he behaves, what he says, what he teaches, how he himself practises. You see how he follows all those precepts that he has taught you. Supposing he gets up early in the morning and does some meditation, you are at liberty to ask, 'Sir, what is that meditation you perform? Can I do it?' If he says you are fit for that, do it along with him. So he is a guide in every respect – he makes his student go through all the necessary steps to achieve the same result that he has achieved. He has followed the path and he has become a teacher now, just like a professor who has undergone some training. Now he is in a position to teach other students. But was he not a student? He was a student, and from his *guru* he learned this *vidya*, this knowledge, wisdom. Now his expertise is such that he can share that knowledge and give it to another person. He should be open, without any reservations or inhibitions, and answer any question that the disciple asks. He must very willingly, lovingly, compassionately teach him everything, not keeping any secret from him. That sort of *guru* is a true *guru*.

Sri Ramana's devotees had tremendous devotion to him and he to Arunachala. Please say something about bhakti, *devotion, in the pursuit of awakening.*

Bhakti is the equivalent of devotion. Devotion always implies devotion to something, towards something; so you are a devotee and there is a deity, a god. You will devote all your time to the deity and you invoke his blessings; you invoke him and you want his grace to flow towards you. You are asking for something. *Bhakti* is always towards a deity who is in a position to grant something that you desire. So in *Vedanta*, even though they are quite different, *bhakti* is definitely equated with *jnana*, which means acquiring knowledge, acquiring intuitive knowledge.

Would you say it's important that the bhakti *and the* jnana *are woven together? Could you say that it's a necessary attitude towards your* guru, *this devotion?*

Instead of saying necessary attitude, we can say that we are devotees from birth. *Bhakti*, a belief in something, is natural in man. It is something which is within your control – you can do *bhakti*, you need not do *bhakti*; you may do it in a different way than it is mentioned in the scriptures. But *jnana* is not like that. *Jnana*, aquiring knowledge, depends on another who has the knowledge. So that is the difference between *bhakti* and *jnana*. *Bhakti* is worshipping God, seeking His grace.

Can it be the guru's *grace? Can the devotion be towards the* guru?

We have a *Sanskrit* verse:
> *Guru Brahma, Guru Vishnu, Guru Devo Maheswara.*
> *Guru sakshat parambrahman tasmayi Sri Gurumay namaha.*

That's the prayer we recite before we start any class. *Guru Brahma* – *guru* himself is the ultimate Reality. Look at how it is: *guru's* position is eulogised. It is praised to such an extent that *guru* himself is a living god before me. You must have that much faith in him. Supposing the disciple doesn't have any trust in the *guru* – the *vidya*, the knowledge that he gets, will be of no consequence.

So then bhakti *is an essential part of the* guru-*disciple relationship?*

Yes, a very essential part, and this is natural. Man, in his nature, is devoted. He has devotion towards his parents, devotion towards his teachers, devotion towards his *guru* or a deity. The scriptures, the priests, tell you to invoke the blessings of this deity and you will get what you desire. So like that, all these things are happening. But the *guru* must be trustworthy, and he should not cheat the student.

Seekers often have curious ideas about the enlightened state. Please describe your typical day and how you perceive the world.

When the seeker gets the final knowledge of the Self there is no change, except his identification is shifted from the ego to the Self. Now he knows the Reality. Formerly he was thinking something was real which was not real. Hence, it was a misconception. Now he has conviction that this is the Reality, and this Reality can never cease to exist. It is eternal, non-dual, beyond time, space, causation, beyond *dharma* and *adharma*, the merits and demerits, all the things that are mentioned in the scriptures. It is something that he can never think of as ceasing to exist. It can never go out of existence. It is the Reality, the One Reality, yet we don't call it One – we say non-dual, absolute, eternal.

So in your typical day are there no special fireworks at all?

No. I can put it this way – when one becomes a *jnani*, one who knows, there is a vast change in his perspective. He is not to be found behaving as others; he is not seeking the society, the company of people. If he seeks company at all it is with like-minded people or the disciples. Otherwise, he keeps to himself, he seeks solitude. That's a symptom even in a *mumukshu* (one whose mind is introverted), before becoming a *jivanmukta*, even at that time he seeks solitude, and what does he do during this solitude? He is always training the mind towards the ultimate Reality.

You have given us a profound discourse on awakening. When you meet someone with a passion for awakening, what would your short advice be?

A true seeker has passion. A true seeker is very devoted; he is prepared to give up everything except this one knowledge. In other words, he is not like the others. He seeks this and this alone. So naturally, we have to tell such a person, 'Seek it from a *guru* who is a *shrutriya brahmanishta* (one who is well versed in the traditional method of teaching and is established in the ultimate Reality) and your success will be very fast.' It will be a short trip to success. He must find a *shrutriya brahmanishta* and find out for himself. He must trust the teacher and get all the experiences here and now so he can experience those things himself.

Thank you. Is there anything else you wish to add to this dialogue?

Approach a *shrutriya brahmanishta* and, from close contact, you can find out if your calibre is good. There need not be any doubt that he will definitely deliver the goods, bring you that sense of conviction after which you will never waver, and you will never have any doubts.

That was so in my case. (starts to cry) When I saw this teacher I got it. I was convinced, and I need not seek anybody else's advice. In fact, a stage has come when I can give advice to others. Such a powerful personality I came across – I was lucky.

You have been brought to tears a few times today.

I don't know. It happens so quickly I have no control over it. It overtakes me because I have done a lot of *bhakti*. I used to cry like a child.

These tears are not the tears of sadness. They are the tears of joy, which is the language of the Self. Thank you.

Radha Ma

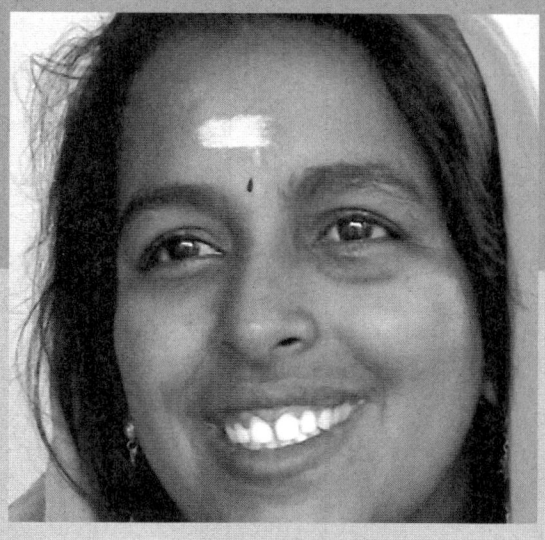

The moment you make a blueprint then you are freezing the moment. The whole awakening is a mystery and the moment you make a blueprint, the beauty is gone. It is different for everybody, a different path and different way, so you can't make a common blueprint.

We are already That,
we are not ignorant to be enlightened.

Radha Ma

Radha Ma

A young woman of unknown age (perhaps early 40s), she originated from Bangalore and she worked successfully for many years in Hyderabad as a chartered accountant. It was here she met her husband and they chose to marry to escape the family marriage pressures. He lived with her as a devotee. She refused to see herself as a *guru* or master but many came to her anyway. Radha Ma left the body in 2011.

Arranging this interview with Radha Ma in 2003 was a delight. She was immediately completely available, saying, 'Why not now?' So we sat together and had lots of fun making the interview. Meeting her again in recent years, there was tremendous love in her presence. The large sign on her gate read: 'I'm not a guru. *Instead of wasting your time trying to meet me, you can go to Ramanashramam.' I was touched that despite this, she accepted my invitations to speak at the Arunachala Pilgrimage Retreat. Her uncompromising delivery of Truth was lovingly and humorously expressed. A wise woman.*

Radha, I am very pleased to be sitting here with you at your home in the shadow of Arunachala in Tiruvannamalai. Before we start the questions, I understand that you have something to say about this title, **Blueprints for Awakening?**

The moment you make a blueprint then you are freezing it, freezing the moment. You see, the whole awakening is a mystery and the moment you make a blueprint, the beauty is gone. You can't make a blueprint as it is not a common thing for everybody. It is different for everybody, a different path and different way, so you can't make a common blueprint.

I agree with you. By approaching different teachers who have different paths or a different experience or kind of awakening, I am asking them to share that, to share their blueprint.

Oh! I don't have one, I was not awakened. (laughs)

So you don't have any blueprint?

Right, because I was not awakened. Because I never slept.

You were always awake?

Yes. Awakening comes, it is a relative term. The moment you sleep the awakening comes, but to the one who has never slept there is no awakening. So the term awakening is meaningless for me. (laughs)

Sri Ramana proposed the fundamental question 'Who am I?' Who are you?

Yes. Ramana proposed the fundamental question for the *sadhakas*, the spiritual seekers, to control the mind, not for the masters, not for the one who is already awake. The moment you asked me 'Who am I?' that is the moment I started describing myself, and sadly the beauty was gone. I started limiting the unlimited and trying to finite the infinite; do you understand? The moment I start saying that I am this and I am that then it's sadly mixed up and looks so ugly. And it's infinite! I can say that I am consciousness, I am this, I am that, but I am none of these. I am not this, I am not that; I am what I am. So this only goes for the spiritual seekers who are trying to figure out who they are, not for the one who knows who he is. (both laugh)

Are you saying you know who you are, and who you are is this moment?

No, I said 'Who am I?' can't be comprehended. It can't be explained. It's the infinite. People can't understand the infinite, so we start using words like 'I am compassionate', 'I am *Brahman* (absolute reality)', 'I am limitless' and 'I am consciousness'. Suppose you changed the term 'consciousness' to 'stupidity' in the dictionary, then I am stupidity too! Consciousness is a dictionary term, and if it is stupidity then I am stupidity! It's the mind trying to comprehend something that can't be comprehended, so these words are needed for that.

You are just who you are at this moment, right? As it is now in this present moment?

Yes, I am ever and the same; I am changeless. If you talk about time, then I am the same whether it is past or present or future; it's me, it's changeless.

Many Western seekers, like the people coming to your Satsang *(meeting in Truth), come to India looking for enlightenment as though it is an experience. What is enlightenment?*

It's a mind game. It is what you call a mind state. Always this mind wants something higher: if it goes to the material world then it wants to be rich, if it goes to the emotional world then it wants to be loved, and in the spiritual world it wants enlightenment. So, always the higher things in the mind states. There is no such thing as enlightenment, there is no such thing as a spiritual seeker, and you are already That. We are already That, we are not ignorant to be enlightened. Ignorance needs the enlightenment; ignorance is the mind and needs the enlightenment. There is no mind; we are not the mind. It's an ego trip, nothing else. If people are unsatisfied with the material world then they try spirituality, only to find that nothing like enlightenment exists.

So my next question is a bit funny because if there is no enlightenment then there are no qualifications for enlightenment. My question is: Are there any qualifications for enlightenment?

Who is here to qualify anybody? Who can say that you and I are qualified to be enlightened? My enlightenment is given, then where does the qualification come from? It's just gross, just a business.

So is it necessary to do some spiritual practices? Is sadhana *(spiritual practice)* necessary?

It is necessary to know that ultimately it's unreal, that there is no enlightenment required. Enlightenment is an illusion; our mind is an illusion. But *sadhana* alone will not bring you that reality. Spiritual practice is needed to know the Truth and to understand the Truth. Suppose you go to a farmer and tell him he is God, he will never believe you and will laugh at you. He needs a basic *sadhana* to understand the ultimate reality, or rather to accept this reality, that this is real. The spiritual seeker, the *sadhaka*, is real, and to know that he needs a *sadhana*. But he does not need that for anything else, not for enlightenment.

So in a way it is useful to be able to get to know the mind, to see the mind and to know that is not who you are. In that way it is useful?

Yes. To know that ultimately mind is an illusion, to understand that. *Sadhana* is not going to bring you the final cut; through *sadhana* you can never lose identification. But to know that as knowledge, as an understanding, then *sadhana* is required.

Is it also necessary to quieten the mind, to have a sattvic *(calm and peaceful)* mind?

Yes. The mind is an illusion but the moment you say it then people can't accept this. They find that they are struggling and fighting with the mind every day. Spiritual practice is required to make your foe into your friend. All these days you are fighting with your mind, and by doing *sadhana* and doing meditation it is going to become your friend. That's it. But still the mind exists and the illusion exists. That's the Truth.

Whether a friend or foe, it is an illusion. The nightmare becomes a sweet dream, that's all, but the dream is continuous.

Sri Ramana said that Self-enquiry is the most direct route to realising the Self. What do you say about Self-enquiry?

I don't know. I never practised Self-enquiry so I can't comment on this. (both laugh) Seriously, this is correct. I never walked on the path so I can't say whether it is right or not. Ramana never practised Self-enquiry either. There was no need for that.

You see what happens? The moment you start 'Who am I?' maybe it helps initially to control the mind, but after some time it becomes an auto suggestion. Then when a thought comes you ask 'Who am I?' and the thought subsides, but you never erase the thought. It becomes an auto suggestion after some time if you don't have a proper understanding.

I think the idea of Self-enquiry is to bring your attention to the part that never changes.

You see, the moment when you reach the final path and you are ready for that awakening, or whatever you call it, then anything will wake you up. It may not be Self-enquiry. It may be surrender, love, devotion; anything will wake you up. Any thought will take you there, once you are ready for that. It is not Self-enquiry alone, it is not the only way.

And when you say 'ready for that', what do you mean?

You do all the *sadhanas* and then you understand this ultimate Truth.

That is what I mean when I ask, 'Are there any qualifications?' I mean is something needed as preparation?

Preparation happens. It need not be this and that, but continuous; it is like beginning college. To get a degree in college, what happens? First you have to go to playschool and go higher and higher and then finally you get your degree. But there is no qualification. No one can decide about the qualification. Nobody can say that somebody from playschool goes directly to college. We are not here to decide it.

We are seeing only one lifetime, only one scene of a movie, and we don't know the rest of the lifetimes, so 'qualifications' is a limited term. You see somebody who meditates for a year and he is enlightened, then you see someone else who has been meditating for forty or fifty years and he didn't get any glimpse of it. So trying to judge the qualifications through this one lifetime is not possible.

In your case you say that you were awakened already?

I never said that I was awakened! (laughs)

You said that you weren't asleep and that you have never been asleep, yes? So you didn't have to awaken. Are you saying this is the result of other parts of your movie, of other lifetimes?

You are trying to make me identify with myself. My last dream is over, I am just awake and you have asked me to identify myself. Which dream shall I identify myself with, the last dream? Or the dream previous to that? I don't have any option and I don't know how to identify myself with any of these things. I am not that, I am not the dream. I am not the dreamer to identify myself with. You are forcing me to tell something about the dreams, but it is all over for me. There is no reason for me to go back and relate myself to any of these dream characters. I am having difficulty can't you see? You are talking about my dream and I don't know which dream I can relate to you.

Right. Your response is very fresh and innocent. If you continue to teach, and lots of Westerners come, you will have to find a teaching and some techniques and then you will have to write some books! (laughs) Then you will need an **ashram**.

Come on! If you are really in Truth then there is no need for any compromise. All these things you are telling, they are all compromise. There is no need to compromise if you are already in this Truth. Nothing matters, so if I tell the Truth and people believe, let them believe. I can't suggest a false method or a false practice for them. The moment I do that, I compromise the Truth, I fall back from the Truth.

But you must already experience that with Western people. When Indian people come they want to worship you and make you the Divine Mother, and when Western people come they want some technique, right? They want to know about enlightenment.

That's true, but I said that enlightenment doesn't exist. You are already unlimited. You are not ignorant to be enlightened. That is the Truth too. I don't find any difference. If I find that you are sleeping or if I find out that you are ignorant then I ought to find a method for you to wake up. But I find that you and I are the same, there is no difference; you are the divine and I am the divine, everybody is the divine here. So there is no need for me to find a practice to suggest to you. You are pretending you are sleeping; you are not really sleeping. There is no reason for me to compromise with the Truth.

As a Western person I am conditioned to do things. My life is all about doing things. I expect I have to do my enlightenment. Do you see?

Sure. But you are conditioned to do it this way.

You will never be successful as a teacher if you tell them it is simply grace!

Success is such a worldly term. The one who stands in the Truth doesn't care for success or failure. It is for the Truth. The Truth is the Truth. If it is accepted then it is accepted, if it is not then it is not. That's it! I have nothing to do; I have no personal motivation in this Truth. I can't make any personal business out of this Truth. Do you see that?

I understand that. I am just provoking you! (both laugh)

There is no need for me to compromise anywhere. It is not me or the personal 'I' that exists to compromise. It's the Truth and non-truth. The Truth decides and there is no need for me to compromise. I no longer exist for any personal benefit. It is the success or failure of the eternal Truth. If it fails then who cares? Let it fail, then it can't be Truth. If it is not being accepted then it can't be Truth. If it is really Truth, if it is eternal, then it should be accepted. It is not my personal failure or success anyway. I don't want to be a master. I don't want to be a *guru*. To say that I am going to be a successful *guru* or not, it does not matter.

When Sri Ramana was asked, 'When will the realisation of the Self be gained?' he replied, 'When the world which is what-is-seen has been removed, there will be realisation of the Self which is the seer.' What is the true understanding of the world?

It is the mind. It is very simple. The world never exists outside our mind. Our mind is the world. The mind created the world. The moment that you identify that there is no mind, you see yourself – that's it! You have identified all these years with the mind; the moment the mind is gone then the world is gone too! The world, that never exists, is the mind.

And how to remove the world?

Now this is what we call *sadhana* or practice. We come back to all those lengthy procedures. Right?

Right.

All these days you are thinking you are X, right? I am telling you, or everybody is telling you, that you are not X but you are A. So how does this identification fall off? You are a prince on the road but throughout your life you are lost, the lost child of a king. You don't know that you are a prince; you are in beggar's garb.

Then one day the king comes and tells you, 'You are not a beggar, you are the prince. You are my lost son.' In that very moment you become the prince, whether you are in the garb of a beggar or not. In your mind you become the prince immediately the king tells you; the identification of the beggar falls off at the same moment.

So why not this? I am telling you that you are not the mind, you are the Self. So why don't you throw this off? It should happen in the same moment. Realisation is as simple as that.

When you say it is as simple as that, do you mean that actually you don't need thirty years of sitting in meditation or singing mantras *(sacred sounds)? You can just see this Truth in any moment?*

Yes.

That I am the Self?

Yes. *Sadhana* is not necessary. Nothing is necessary to see this Truth, but to accept this Truth needs *sadhana*. Suppose the king comes and says, 'You are my son,' then you will believe it. Suppose somebody else says, 'You are not the beggar, you are the lost child of the king, you are the prince.' You will not accept that. The spiritual practice is needed for the acceptance, not for the Truth. We should accept somebody's words; that needs *sadhana*.

It has been suggested that the mind must be destroyed for liberation to occur. Do you have a mind?

No, no. The mind is illusion. The mind does not exist anymore. I don't know what mind is.

You say that you don't have mind; if you got in a car then you could drive the car, right? When you worked as a tax officer you could work with computers and with figures and calculations, right? So for doing those kinds of things you need a mind.

Sure, also I have a point of view to answer all these questions and I should have a dictionary in my mind to speak all these words, right? But it comes spontaneously from consciousness, from my inner being. It's not through the mind. Mind always manipulates, judges; nothing of this happens here. Before I answer a question I don't have to think whether I am right or wrong, nothing like that. That is the problem with the mind. The mind always calculates and manipulates, but when something comes from spontaneity – the mind never existed here. I don't know whether I am right or wrong from your point of view, I don't care about it either. There is no judgement, nothing. It just happens.

When you say you don't have a mind, do you mean that you don't have the memories, experiences, worries, conditionings and knowledge that society and teachers gave you? Are you saying that you have a mind in the sense you can do things when you need to, to operate your body?

Yes, that has been taken care of, but there have also been so many days that I have lived without food. I am beyond the physical and beyond the mental, the mind cannot be here now. All these emotions and attachments are transcended. I don't want to say that I am different; the moment I say that I don't have mind I feel I am different from you. It feels ugly to say it, but it is true.

Could you say, 'I am not attached to my mind'?

No, there is no mind at all to be attached to! Attachment is a different thing. I don't have a mind at all, it does not exist, it's an illusion. And once you cut off that illusion, where does it come from? There is no mind at all. It is just an illusion.

Are you telling me that since you were very young you never really had a mind? You never really lived in your thoughts?

No. No thoughts. I don't know how to explain it more than that. I didn't have words to explain those stages. I was what I was. Maybe what

I was when I was a child and what I am today are the same. There is no difference in me, I am the same. So what you say about the mind is relative. I don't find that the world or mind exist for me, but as the body is in the world, you think I am in the world. And because I talk, you think that I have mind too. Apparently it looks like that, but it is not.

When you worked in the tax office it looked like you had a mind to do these complicated calculations.

Nothing of the sort. It is being taken care of. In fact I didn't study much about these things. I didn't even study computers. The moment I wanted to learn about computers I went to a hardware training institute. My lecturers objected. They told me, 'You are a tax consultant and don't have any electronics background so we can't teach you. You need some electronics background.'

But after a few days it was as if I knew the subject best in the class. I was even correcting the master; I told him that he was wrong in so many things. He was really shocked and he thought that I had learned it somewhere else and that I was there teasing him. (both laugh) This really happened, I am not joking! Actually they thought that I had learned it somewhere else and was coming to class to annoy these people, but I was not. The moment I had made the decision to learn it, the knowledge came to me.

Then I found that there is no need for me to learn anything. Whether in this world or another world there is no need to learn. Everything is already available. When you use a computer you use a server. I am a client, so I receive whatever record is being sent by the server – that's what happens. The ultimate takes care of that. I don't have anything of my own, just a monitor is enough. So whatever the server sends, the client receives it, that's it! I need not have a CPU (central processing unit) of my own.

When Western people come with their minds, their sufferings, their worries, tensions and fears, can you understand immediately that this is an illusion, that this is not true? What do you say to them?

Whether a person is Western or Indian, all suffering and pain are illusions. You are dreaming and you believe that you are having a nightmare; you dream that a tiger is chasing you, but it is an illusionary tiger and illusionary fear too. Any suffering, whether it is Western or Indian or whatever, is like that; all suffering is illusion. You imagine you suffer, that's it. There is no suffering really. Everything is perfect in you.

Everything is exactly as it should be!

Yes, it is perfect. I can say that you are dreaming. I can say it one hundred and one times but still you dream and still you are frightened of the tiger; you can't help it, because it is perfect and it should be like that.

You yourself will wake up from the dream one day and see that all those times you were chased and frightened by an imaginary tiger! But everything is perfect. It is perfect for you to be afraid now. It is perfect for you to have the nightmare now. We can't say that it is wrong, it is perfect.

Are you saying that you accept whatever comes, whether it be happy or unhappy, sad, angry or blissful?

Mind is illusion, so why are you bothered if mind is angry or not, or whether it is jealous or suspicious? The mind itself is illusory, so why should you be bothered by this negative quality of the mind? Everything is perfect. Mind is like this. Mind can be angry or peaceful, mind can be happy or unhappy. But it is illusion. How to say something is good or something is bad in the illusion? This illusion is illusion, it is still illusion, and it is perfect whatever comes.

What do you say to somebody that comes to you? You tell them that it is an illusion, but still they are suffering and they come every day to see you with this pain. The pain is there from something which they believe so strongly that they can't just throw it away. What do you say to them?

I say the same thing to them: it is all perfect! You suffered, it's perfect. You trusted, it's perfect. So many people seek in the world and then come back. They say, 'We have meditated for ten years and we didn't get it,' and they are frustrated. And this frustration is perfect. I can say that your seeking is a waste, but this is not real for you. My knowledge and my Truth is not real for you, it is not your Truth; you have to find out your own Truth.

So I say this, 'What you are seeking is stupidity, there is no enlightenment,' but still your mind can't accept that. You meditate for one week and there is no enlightenment, so the mind says 'Why should I meditate?' So you stop meditating and then next week the mind comes back and says, 'What you are doing is rubbish. You have to sit and meditate.'

That's what the mind says, so you follow the mind. It is that which is going to give you the happiness, not me! My Truth is mine and your Truth is yours and until you find out the Truth for yourself you have to walk on the path.

Suppose you start off from home and I say that this is your home and that you need not travel anywhere; you can't accept this, you have to travel, you have to get fed up and be frustrated and come back to the same place and realise that this is the home from where you actually started. It's perfect. You have to find out for yourself. It is the mind, that is what the mind is.

But you are also telling the people that it is just grace, that in a way they cannot do anything!

You see there is no other way to tell them, right? Grace is just a word we use. Grace is not outside us, grace is us, we are the grace. They say, 'I waited, what to do?' Or 'Why does grace happen to somebody else and not to me?' I say that it is just like a fruit on a tree: the moment it ripens it falls from the tree and until then you have to wait for that. If you are not falling that means that you are not ripe enough!

Grace is a word and there is no other way to express that waiting. Ultimately everybody is reaching the same place so there is nothing to worry about. It's perfect. Today it's me and tomorrow somebody else. So it doesn't make any difference. It is not through my own effort that I am in this state. It's the Ultimate that is taking care of me, and it takes care of everything. So the Ultimate Reality, which is Truth for me, is Truth for you too. It takes care of you too.

Even me? (both laugh) Even me with my favourite sufferings? Even me?

Why not you? (both laugh) Why not you?

Because I am not worthy!

Then I am not also. I am a fellow unworthy person.

I think that this sense of unworthiness…

It comes from the mind.

Right, it is just mind. It's a very common thought.

It's a very tricky mind! Suppose you corner it with, 'I am not worthy,' then it will say, 'Oh, no! I am most worthy! I did meditation for so many years. I am most eligible.' If you go positive then the mind will take the negative stand and if you go to the negative it will then take the positive stand. That's it.

I am very glad I brought a video camera because many times you say something and I can feel it in the silence around what you say with words. The way you look, smile, laugh and also the way you do nothing.
    What about vasanas, *the tendencies of the mind? Must these be removed before Self-realisation can become permanent?*

Okay, (laughs) when you are talking about *vasanas*, who is having the *vasanas*? The mind is having the *vasanas* and it has nothing to do with

Self-realisation. The mind itself is an illusion, and what are the *vasanas*? They are another part of the illusion. Maybe the moment you know you are the Self and that the mind is an illusion, the *vasanas* never existed.

But there is a certain quality about vasanas. *I can say from my own experience that for a number of years I haven't had much mind.*

There is no 'much mind'. Either you have a mind or you don't have a mind. You can't say that you don't have 'much mind'. It's the wrong word. Either you are in the mind or you are not in the mind. That's it.

Well, I am English so I am rather modest! (both laugh) Okay, I can say that I haven't had a mind for a few years now. But still there are times when the mind is there and when I look I see certain patterns again and again. In my case two strong patterns have been coming up for my whole life. So even though I can say that I don't have a mind, I still can say that I have some kind of mind-storm. Everything is calm and suddenly a vasana *will come. It will be the conditioning of the mind, it will be some silly pattern that seems to recur, what I am calling a* vasana *or tendency. It has a very persistent quality.*

I know a number of people who spent time with Papaji. He had a very powerful energy and many woke up to the Self. They would go away and come back saying, 'I have lost it.' Many of them had this experience with vasanas *pulling them out of that awakening. Can you say something about* vasanas *in this context?*

If *vasanas* still exist that means that you are in the mind, you are not out of the mind. The moment you have lost the true identity, even if you have had a glimpse of it, the moment it is lost, it is lost forever. The moment you find it is illusory, then the mind no longer exists for you. The mere fact that you are saying you still have *vasanas* means you are still in the mind. Maybe you have a much quieter and friendlier mind; maybe the mind is even your slave and you may even be the master of the mind, but still the mind exists for you because *vasanas* exist for you.

Once you get it there is no way of losing it, if truly you got it. You know the mind has created the world; all creation is from the mind so it is easy for the mind to create hundreds of enlightenments too. You get such praise, happiness and feel almost enlightened, but after some time the mind comes back. That's the reason, because it happens in the mind. Some parts of the mind are agitated and very aggressive and angry but some parts are so peaceful, just like the ocean; but still it happens in the mind.

You are saying that you can feel, 'Oh! I am awake,' but the awakening is still in the mind, it is not beyond the mind.

Awakening happens only in the mind because mind is waking and wants awakening. Awakening is a term related to the mind, not to us, not to Self. The moment you say you are awakened it happens in the mind. It's not the Truth. The moment you say you are awakened, that means you were sleeping all those days; it is the mind who sleeps to wake up. If you are really the Truth, and if you lost identification with the mind and know you are the true Self, then there is no awakening and enlightenment for you. This happens in the mind. The moment you talk about *vasanas* it is still happening in the mind. The mind is the one that was born with the *karma* (result of all action); it is an illusion. *Karma* and *vasanas* are total illusion. The moment you talk about it, and it is real to you, then the mind is real to you too.

All those days you have tied yourself with a rope. It's all illusion, you are free. That's it. If you feel that the rope is hurting you here and there, that means that you are bound with an illusionary rope. There is no bondage for the one who is free. The moment you find that the rope is illusion, you cannot find any bruises on your body. So the moment you find that mind is an illusion, then you can't find *vasanas* anymore; *vasanas* are like the bruises.

If you say 'I still have the bruises on my body,' that means that you still have the ropes on your body. You still think that the ropes are real to you. The rope is imaginary!

At the end of his book, Self-Enquiry, *Sri Ramana says, 'He who is thus endowed with a mind that has become subtle and who has the experience of the Self is called a* jivanmukta.' *Is this the state that can be called Self-realised? He goes on, 'And when one is immersed in the ocean of bliss and has become one with it without any differentiated existence, one is called a* videhamukta. *It is this state of* videhamukti *that is referred to as the transcendent* turiya *(state). This is the final goal.' Is this the state that can be called enlightenment?*

I don't believe in enlightenment at all. So this question becomes irrelevant. I don't believe in enlightenment and awakening. The mind was ignorant and needed to be enlightened, right?

Are you saying that there cannot be Self-realisation and enlightenment, there is not even anything?

These are just names given to identify the mind and cross beyond it. These are just words. The moment I say that you are enlightened, or that enlightenment is there, that means I am limiting you, I am saying that you are ignorant and need to be enlightened. The moment I say that you are awake and talk about your awakening, that means that I am limiting you to sleeping now. That is stupidity! You are not sleeping; you are imagining that you are sleeping. You are not sleeping. Do you see the difference? So I don't believe in this enlightenment at all.

So you certainly don't believe in any stages of enlightenment?

No stages. There are no stages; stages always belong to the mind. These stages, procedures, methods, successes and failures, whatever you call them, are relevant to the mind, not to the Self. The Self is beyond all these things. You cannot have a stage in the Self; that's it. How can you put stages in this?

Swami Shivananda from Rishikesh is a famous saint. He has a book where he talks about the seven stages of enlightenment...

Suppose I tell something about a particular place beyond this hill but you can't understand because you see only the hill and not beyond it. So maybe to take you beyond the hill somebody says, 'Okay, you go up this hill and then you can see that.' But if you go up the hill, then they say, 'If you cross the hill, then you can see this.'

This is a way to make you walk. If they say that this is a hundred kilometres from here then you will be fainting. So they say, 'Okay, you should walk twenty kilometres and then you will see a tree and there you will get the guidance.'

You walk that twenty kilometres and then the guidance says you should walk another twenty kilometres and you will find somebody else and that will be the end of it. So you walk the whole hundred kilometres like this. It is a way to make you walk. Don't think about it. All these are just tricks to make you interested in this, to take you beyond this. It is a way to make the people move, it is a practice.

You are saying that because Swami Shivananda had an **ashram** *he needed a teaching and then he needed a book? (both laugh)*

I don't care what he says. He is a master and he knows what he does. We are trying to find out something that can't be found out. That is the difficulty for all the people, right? You want to comprehend something that is beyond the mind, and through the mind you try to comprehend it. It is beyond the mind and it is very difficult. He is a master in his own right and he knows what he does.

In bookshops you find a whole section of spiritual books and they are full of all these kinds of things, like seven stages of enlightenment. So what you are saying is that all these books are nonsense because they are attempting to say what is on the other side of the mountain?

I know what you are doing. You are trying to fix me up! (laughs) Okay. But I don't believe in these stages. You are That. And who can create stages in the Self? I don't want to ridicule the books or the authors I don't know, but certainly I feel that the Truth to me is that there are no stages. Who fixes the stages? There are no stages. Either you are yourself or you are not; either you are in the mind or you are not in the mind; that's it. Some people say, 'I am so close to that.' There is no close. There is nothing close to the Truth.

You have to promise me that when I come back to interview you in ten years you don't have any stages, okay? (both laugh) I shall come in the back of the crowd and shout out, 'Hey, what about stages?'

Who knows, maybe people will say that I was never in any of the stages. 'She is in playschool and didn't reach any stage,' but I am still going to talk in the same way. They will say, 'She didn't even reach the first stage, and there are a hundred stages!'

Right. They probably will say that.

That's true.

You will need a book I think. Maybe your husband can write it, with stages. (both laugh)

Him write about me? What stupidity! What is he going to write about? The past? It's stupidity! The dream is over so what is the point writing about those dreams? It is all over for me, nothing matters now, nothing. I say that whatever he writes, that it's all false! He can't write about me anyway. (John David laughs) That's true. What I experienced he doesn't know. What I am, he doesn't know. He can't write about that, only I can. But the moment I start writing it becomes so ugly and full of falsehood. The moment I start explaining this, all that I am saying to you, and all of your ten questions, it's all false; it's not true. That's it. That's the Truth. The moment I start to explain the unexplainable, the moment I start reducing it into words, then it loses its beauty. It loses its Truth. Truth can't be told.

I completely agree with what you say. That is really true.

But you say you want to write a book. (laughs) You are close to Truth, maybe? Can we say that you are close to Truth? (laughs)

At the beginning of the book we can write, 'This is all rubbish, don't buy this book.'

Now that is the way to sell your book, you are an intelligent businessman now! (laughs) People will become all the more interested the moment you talk about rubbish. If you say that it is all Truth and tell them to buy it, they won't buy it. But the moment you say that it is all rubbish, then they will buy it.

Do you think that is a good technique?

Yes! (both laugh)

I think this will be a bestseller because your answers are very spontaneous and fresh. It is very beautiful.

So you think that after ten years I will lose my freshness?

Possibly, possibly. We will see. I will come and knock on the door of your **ashram**...

Oh come on, I don't think I will have one.

No?

Ashrams are like cages, limiting the masters. I am a free bird and I don't want to limit myself anymore. So the moment I have an *ashram* I have to compromise the Truth, and I have to find some practice to teach people, to earn money.

Right, you will need a big practice hall, and then you will need some practices.

Yes, the way to enlightenment; I will have to teach them in ten stages! (both laugh)

You could become famous by saying that there is no enlightenment, there are no steps and there are certainly no stages!

I don't want to become famous like that. It is the Truth that I feel. Maybe I will become famous too, but who cares about it?

In fact it is a good book title. After this book I can do a new one called **No Enlightenment, No Stages, No Anything.**

No mind first.
    Somebody talked to me today about killing the ego. I said that is illusion. It is the ego that says, 'Kill me!' It's one of the ego trips too. It is a new phrase that the ego likes. Ego itself is illusion.

So now here is a perfect question for you. It appears essential to meet a **guru** *and to stay with that* **guru**. *Who is the* **guru** *and what is the* **guru's** *role? How to recognise a true* **guru**?

I never had a *guru* so I don't know how to answer this. And also I am not a *guru* either.

Do you think that it is important to have a **guru**?

Yes and no. It all depends. Some people are like children and they need the physical presence of a *guru*. But people who are already strong and independent enough don't need a *guru*. So I can't say whether you need a *guru* or you don't need a *guru* as it all depends on the individual's growth and strength. It can be *karma* too. This question depends on the individual and there is no common answer for this.
    If you are really seeking a *guru*, the moment you meet your *guru* you know that he is your *guru*, that's it. The *guru* is the one who never identifies himself as the *guru*. The *guru* doesn't say, 'I am a great master

and I am here to teach you.' No true *guru* will say that. The moment that you meet a true *guru* and you become a disciple there is a difference, right? You make the difference. It's all the same because a *guru* never finds anybody else. There are no others for him.

When you stop your seeking and go to your *guru* and say, 'I am in ignorance, enlighten me,' the *guru* never finds that you are in ignorance. He knows that you just have the illusion that you are ignorant. So he never says, 'I am your *guru* and I am here to save you.' No true *guru* will say that. He never finds anybody else in the world; it is he who exists everywhere.

So the moment you make a *guru*-disciple relationship, it is always the disciple who makes the relationship, not the *guru*. For the *guru* there is no relationship because he never thinks of himself as the *guru*. The moment I say that I am the *guru* and you are the disciple, the Truth has vanished. The moment I say, 'I have the capacity to teach,' then the Truth has gone.

What I understand from talking with you is that it is just this moment now, it is just this very fresh moment. I can say that my whole experience of meeting you is like this.

I turned up at your house, you came out and then after a few minutes I said, 'How about an interview and a video?' and you said yes. It was so uncomplicated. Everything is simple. That is what I experience with you. It is simple and easy and you just decided in the moment. I was ready to come next week but now is the moment. You just do it now. And in the end it is just like that.

I don't know how it happened. It is happening, that is all.

Seekers often have curious ideas about the enlightened state. Please describe your typical day and how you perceive the world.

I never existed, I exist everywhere. Who is sitting in front of me and asking questions? There are no others here, only I exist here. Nobody else. If you want more humility, then I can say that God exists. If you don't like the term 'I', then we can say you are God and everything is God here. This I is very confusing for most people. They ask if it is a small I or a big I. (laughs) So we use the word God. God exists here, there is nothing else. It is single, there are not many here. This God exists here and that is it. You are God and I am God, rays of the same source. There is no difference at all. I don't find any difference.

I experience that you are mostly in peace. Are there also times when you feel very sad or angry or experience any other kinds of feelings?

I don't think that any of these strong feelings exist for me. I am laughing when I am scolding or am angry with someone else; that is the Truth, I enjoy that. But there is no real anger in that. This real anger I don't get unless someone really needs it. It is just a way of correcting people that need it, that's it. There is nothing there to be angry with. Everything is perfect so I don't feel any of these strong emotions. Everything I enjoy, being angry too. It's fine.

What about the leela, *the divine play? Is your life a kind of* leela?

It is a divine play, a *leela* only. It's only fun.

Only fun, whether you are having fun with anger or with bliss?

Fun itself is bliss. Bliss is fun. Realise nothing but the bliss.

Anger is also fun?

Anger is what those people perceive. So I say something harshly, change the tone, and they say that I am angry. It is not that I am angry. It is not an emotion. There is no anger.

If I talk like this (speaking softly) then the world interprets that I am talking softly and gently, but the moment I raise my voice then they say, 'Yes, she is angry.' It is what you perceive, it is not my actions. It is your idea, it is your reaction to my action, but there is no real anger. If

I am talking in a loud voice then you say, 'Oh! She is angry.' It is not Truth. It never happens because I don't want to talk in a loud voice. I know people who do that. No others exist for me but still they have a mind, so I can't be harsh to them. No other strong emotions for me, except fun. My whole life was full of this so many times. I found it a real problem for others. Maybe for my husband too!

All the time I was having fun. Nothing was serious in my life. The *leela*, as you call it, is so much in my life. (both laugh) Everything is fun.

Before we finish, is there anything else you would like to add?

Now you have all the answers maybe you would have prepared different questions! (both laugh) Am I not right?

Would you like me to find some other questions for you? Is there something we missed?

No. Did we miss something? Only you know.

Thank you.

Thank you too!

Swami Satchidananda

Ramana wants us to find out who we really are. His question, 'Who am I?' is to clarify that we are not the body, mind, intellect and senses, but the Self.
If we realise that, we have realised everything.

We are eternal; we are deathless and we are birthless.

Swami Satchidananda

Swami Satchidananda

After a period of trials and struggles in his early life, Satchidananda met Papa Ramdas when he was thirty. He became a *sannyasin* and, having served Papa Ramdas until he left his body, he assisted Mataji Krishnabai in running Ananda Ashram in North Kerala. In 1989, when Mataji left the body, Satchidananda inherited the mantle of running the *ashram*. True to the divine wish of beloved Papa and Mataji, Swamiji, with his exemplary qualities, became the guiding spirit of the *ashram*. He left the body in 2008.

Swami Satchidananda was a man of unconditional love. We met one quiet evening in 2003 and spent a beautifully intimate time together making this interview. In the years that followed, I brought many to meet him and all were touched by his grace. I was profoundly touched that it was he who gave me my former name **Premananda** *– unconditional love.*

Swami, Sri Ramana proposed the fundamental question, 'Who Am I?' Can I ask you, who are you?

I am not sure if I am capable of dealing with Ramana Maharshi's teachings, all the same I shall try. Ramana Maharshi's approach is direct. He always puts the question, 'Who am I?' This answers all the questions. If we understand what we are, we have nothing more to ask.

We identify ourselves with the body, mind, intellect and senses; that is a wrong identification. Actually we are the Self, that which controls all these things. Ramana wants us to find out who we really are. His question, 'Who am I?' is to clarify that we are not the body, mind, intellect and senses, but the Self. If we realise that, we have realised everything.

Can I ask who you are?

I am That. (both laugh)

That is the correct answer, thank you! Many Western seekers come to India looking for enlightenment as if it is an experience. What is enlightenment?

Enlightenment: we can call it the realisation of the Self. We are in a state of darkness, we are groping in darkness, we want to see light. How to get into this light? We are actually light ourselves, only we have forgotten what we really are. Self-enquiry will lead us to that light. To know ourselves is enlightenment.

Are there any qualifications for enlightenement?

The qualification for enlightenment is absolute purity of the mind. When the mind becomes absolutely pure, the mind as such does not exist. Then enlightenment comes. The mind, with all its dirt, thoughts and *vasanas* (tendencies of the mind), is standing in the way of our knowing what we really are. If the mind is made perfectly pure then we are face-to-face with the Truth, or rather we are one with the Truth.

Would you suggest a period of sadhana *(spiritual practice) to purify the mind?*

Of course. There are various methods and various *sadhanas*. Our master, Ramdas, and other teachers say that if we take up chanting the name of God it will gradually cleanse the mind of all its dirt and make it pure. With the pure mind we can see the light of God. When we first take up this chanting we feel that God is separate from us, we give Him a separate personality and we consider ourselves as His children, His servants, or something different from Him.

This type of devotion, solely to Him, will purify the mind. We consider Him as our mother or our master, we serve Him and dedicate our life entirely to Him, and we think about Him day and night. Whatever we do, we do for His sake, and whatever we think it must be about Him. Moreover we consider that everything is Him in different forms, this way we will be immersed in thoughts of Him only. This constant thinking of Him will perfectly purify our mind and prepare us for His revealing Himself in us. That is the easiest and safest *sadhana*, as prescribed by our master.

In fact, he did that sadhana *himself for a number of years.*

Yes. I just put it in a simple way, but the chanting of God's name gradually makes us feel His presence within us and without us, everywhere. You start feeling His presence everywhere, that He alone is in every action and that His power is absolute. That will help us understand that anything happening in the universe, through this body or that body or any other body, is happening by His will alone; it is a perfect surrender to His will. Master used to say that constant remembrance of God and perfect surrender to His will creates God-realisation.

So the ego, in the sense that it is separate, simply melts away?

That's right. The ego has no place there. When God is in the picture, ego disappears. As long as we are in intense remembrance of God, ego cannot enter, it disappears through the back door. But when we stop remembering Him it enters again. (both laugh)

Would you say that a spiritual ego eradicates the ordinary ego?

In the final stage we can say that it is the spiritual ego, but in the other stages it is the troublesome ego which is an obstruction to our realising God. But the spiritual ego also has to disappear when our mind is perfectly purified and when we don't want it anymore.

Having realised our oneness with God we do maintain a sort of ego, our individuality, but it is perfectly purified and absolutely harmless. It is purely for the sake of playing this game, this *leela* (divine play) of God.

After realisation you know your position as a child, look upon God as your mother and happily engage yourself in day-to-day activities.

Hearing you say this, I feel very blessed in deciding to make this project – meeting and speaking with great masters. I find that each one is expressing God, and yet each does it in their own very individual way. It's the same Truth but experienced and described in different, unique ways.

That's true, because God is infinite. He is a diamond of many facets. We only see Him through one facet and we can only explain about this one facet. People experience Him in different ways and express these different experiences in their own language. And nobody can say that we have understood Him completely because He is infinite.

You mention leela, *divine playfulness. Could you say something more about* leela?

That is the way devotees look at the world. They do not consider the world as an illusion or non-existent, they consider the world to be God playing His eternal drama. He has assumed innumerable forms to play this drama: He Himself is every player. And in the innumerable parts that He has taken, He has assumed individuality in every form. He forgets that He is Himself in these different forms, because of *maya* (illusion of the conditional world), His own illusionary power. So He plays this eternal drama taking innumerable parts Himself. And who is the witness to this great drama? He Himself is the witness, and His drama goes on eternally. That is the way that devotees look upon it.

We see before us concrete forms and we cannot deny that they exist; we have to deal with them. So we appreciate what the devotees say about the *leela* of God. But *jnanis* (ones who have realised the Self), those who have been following the path of Self-enquiry, say that He doesn't exist at all, that He is just a creation of the mind.

The game is ever changing, what happens this minute is different to what happens the next minute. It is an eternally changing game.

Would you say that the world is a war between good and evil, and the divine leela *plays through both?*

It is the divine *leela* only. In the divine *leela* everything is permitted. In the drama we have tragedies and comedies and we appreciate every part played. If one person plays the part of a robber and he does it well, when he comes out of the drama we can congratulate him, 'Oh! You have done your part very well!' In this *leela* everything is possible and everything is necessary.

The question will arise: Why should there be suffering in the world? And the answer is: Who is suffering? If we find out who we are then there is no suffering. Say someone is playing the part of a robber and a policeman comes along and shoots him; the robber falls down on the stage; is he really dying? It affects only the external body, not his soul.

We are eternal; we are deathless and we are birthless. We have taken a body which has a birth and grows, which becomes a corpse and decays. What happens? The body doesn't affect us really, this is why it is called the eternal *leela* of God.

There are different answers about the existence of the world. Some call it illusion and some call it a manifestation of God. God Himself manifests in different forms. They say the forms are consciousness solidified. Like an iceberg. What is an iceberg? It is water in a different form, solidified. This is called ice; it is not different.

So the universe of names and forms is not different from the Self, or Truth or reality. He Himself appears as names and forms, the names and forms are not different from Him just as the ice is not different from water. That is why they say that everything is God. In the scriptures they say, *sarvam kavitam brahman*, everything is *Brahman* (absolute reality), there is nothing but *Brahman*. Because of ignorance we see them as diverse things, but when our vision is purified, we see them as forms of God Himself.

Sri Ramana said that Self-enquiry is the most direct method to realise the Self. What do you say about Self-enquiry? I understand that here in your ashram *the focus is on devotion.*

Self-enquiry is one approach, it is a direct approach, but there are other methods too, like the path of devotion. There are many types of devotion. In our case we chant the names of God. We say *Om Sri Ram, Jay Ram, Jay Jay Ram*. *Ram* stands for the Supreme Being, *Om* is the Supreme Being that is everything and beyond everything. *Ram* is the substratum for this manifestation and *Sri* is the manifestation itself, the power of manifestation. So *Om Sri Ram* covers everything: the Supreme Being, the sub-stratum for the manifestation and the manifestation itself.

When we are chanting *Ram Ram*, we are thinking of the Supreme Being and all that is beyond everything. When we keep thinking that, our mind is taken away from all worldly thoughts and becomes perfectly purified. The purpose of our spiritual practice is only for purifying our mind, taking away all the dirt that has been accumulated over the ages.

So when a person chants sincerely does there come a time when the mind empties and becomes sattvic *(calm and peaceful)*?

Yes, yes. They should do it with concentration, that is important you see. The chanting alone is not sufficient, they must do it with love, devotion and concentration. We chant the name but our mind may be thinking of something else. That is why they say that when you are chanting the name you must keep the mind fixed on the attributes of God. That He is all-pervading, that He has become the entire universe, that He transcends everything and that He is seated in everybody's heart; these are the attributes of God. We can also say that He is all love, all compassion and all mercy.

These things must be working in our minds so that our minds do not stray from the path or think about material things. If this is done the progress will be very fast and the mind will become very pure.

And when somebody stops doing the chanting, does their mind come back?

It comes back until it is perfectly purified. When it is perfectly purified then it has nothing to think of and it can stay quiet for quite a long time. We are all trying to attain this stillness of the mind, it is in the still mind that God reveals Himself.

When Sri Ramana was asked, 'When will the realisation of the Self be gained?' he replied, 'When the world which is what-is-seen has been removed, there will be realisation of the Self which is the seer.' What is the true understanding of the world?

The world we see now is full of diversity. We must practise seeing the unifying force, the unifying spirit that is the substratum for this entire manifestation. That is the Self, the reality, God, or whatever name you may give it. Just like in the cinema the wide screen is the substratum for this manifestation, and what is going on here in this universe is the film, the moving picture. It is always moving but the screen is permanent, just as the substratum is permanent.

If we know that what we see in the world is moving and if we find that which is not moving, then we have realised the Truth and we do not see the world as such. We see it only as a moving thing within the unmoving or immutable existence. Then the world has a different shape for us, we don't see it as diversity, we see it as one.

Jnanis do not say that they don't see the world. They are moving, they are seeing, they are talking, they are talking to others, they cannot say that they don't see the world at all. They see the world but they don't see it as the world. They see it as moving names and forms on the immutable existence. Devotees use another language: they see the world as God Himself.

Our master, Ramdas, wrote a book; he called it *World is God*. Others see the world as world, but saints see the world as God.

How to remove the world?

We don't remove the world. We see the substratum, which we see is God, and we see the world as God. The world as world is removed and the world as God remains. The world does not change. Except of course when we sit in sacred *samadhi* (absorption in the Self). When we sit in meditation we lose our body consciousness and merge with the unmanifest aspect of God for a short while. We merge with our own Self. There the world does not exist for us. But when we come back to world consciousness we see the world, and at that same time we maintain that stillness and peace absolute. This is the state of all the saints. The world does not run away from us, the world is still very much with us but in a different form.

This is a very important statement because it has been suggested that the mind must be destroyed for liberation to occur.

It is not destroying the mind, it is purifying the mind. When the mind is purified of all the dirt, the tendencies and the desires, it is *atman* (the individual aspect of the Self) itself.

Can I ask you, do you have a mind?

I have not become a *jivanmukta* (liberated soul in this life) yet. (both laugh)

Nobody here will believe you.

It's a fact! When the thoughts completely disappear and the mind is completely immersed in God, then we can say that we have realised the Truth. But until then we have no authority to say that.

How to destroy the mind? Self-enquiry is one of the best spiritual practices prescribed, or we can chant the name of God. With this practice, purification takes place: all the thought waves disappear and the mind becomes perfectly pure. It is not destroying the mind, it is purifying the mind.

What about vasanas, *the tendencies of the mind*?

They all have to go before we can realise the Truth, they are the dirt accumulated during the ages.

Do you mean that these vasanas *have come with us into this life?*

We must have accumulated them for ages. We come with all those *vasanas* and we may add some more and carry them forward, and it goes on until the whole thing is destroyed.

And how to destroy the vasanas*?*

When we have made the mind pure and realised that we are one with absolute Truth, then the *vasanas* are all destroyed. This is the only way.

So in a sense it is a constant purification?

Yes, it is a constant struggle to keep the mind perfectly pure.

At the end of his book, Self-Enquiry, *Sri Ramana says, 'He who is thus endowed with a mind that has become subtle and who has the experience of the Self is called a* jivanmukta.' *Is this the state that can be called Self-realised?*

That's right, it's called Self-realised.

He goes on 'And when one is immersed in the ocean of bliss and has become one with it without any differentiated existence one is called a videhamukta.'

As far as I understand, they say *jivanmukta* is a soul realised while in the body and *videhamukta* is a soul realised at the time of leaving the body. I may be right or I may be wrong, but as far as I understand this is the difference.

Death alone does not liberate. Death of this particular body does not give us liberation; what has to die is the ego. The physical form, the mind, intellect and senses, all these bodies must go, and only then are we fully liberated. But when this physical body dies we carry the other bodies with us; the astral body, the mind and the intellect. We are not completely dead, we have only dropped one part of our body, so we are not liberated souls.

And then we take up another body?

Until we take up another body we remain as the subtle body, the astral body. Then we come back as a child and bring back with us all that we have accumulated in previous births; we grow up and work these things out in our life.

How can we tell who is a **jivanmukta** *and who is not a* **jivanmukta**?

It is difficult for others to understand, it is difficult for us.

We would all say that you are a **jivanmukta** *yet you say you are not.*

That's right. It is difficult for others to understand. We ourselves don't know if this is the case or not the case.

Can you give some guidelines for this state of **jivanmukti**?

The guidelines are these: when we know that we are the all-pervading reality and we are one with everything in the universe, when we are no longer bound by the ego, then we have become *jivanmukta*s and we are realised souls. But when we see another person as different to us, 'Oh! I am nothing to do with him!' then we are in the small self, the ego-controlled life. That is not *mukti* or *jivanmukti*, that is ignorance.

We have to get out of ignorance, break out of the small self and embrace the entire universe and beyond as our own. We can know ourselves, it is not difficult. A bird in a cage knows that he is in a cage, but when the cage is open he flies about and enjoys freedom. This we can enjoy.

As I have been travelling to make these interviews the teachers I meet seem to have some common attributes. There is availability, a stillness and peacefulness, even a playfulness, a leela *about them which seems to set them aside from other people.*

Yes. This is naturally so when they are one with the entire universe; these teachers are not bound by the ego and all the pairs of opposites that had been troubling them. They are not affected by the play of God in the universe, so they take everything easy. Suppose you come and abuse me, why should your words affect me? I am unaffected by all these things. I am not burned by fire, water cannot wet me. I am the Self.

They say that Buddha had so much patience that when somebody started abusing him, using filthy language, he just continued smiling. And when his abuser's vocabulary was exhausted, Buddha said:

'My dear friend, suppose you offer me an apple and I don't accept it, where will it be?'

'The apple will remain with me.'

Buddha said, 'So whatever you have said, I do not accept it.'

They have that much patience. They don't feel that abuse, or anything else, in any way affects them because they are identifying themselves with the Self only, whereas we are identifying ourselves with the body. That is the only difference.

So when you see me sitting here, do you see me as the Self?

We see the body plus the substratum. We see that everything in the universe is based on the substratum that is Self. So when we are progressing on the path our vision gradually changes, and when we are finally established in the Self we are completely changed.

Are you saying there is a gradual movement into the depth of the Self?

That's right, according to the purification of our mind. When we wear very dark glasses everything we see is dark. As the tint becomes gradually less and less, slowly we see everything clearer. When our vision is perfectly clear we realise the Truth and we see everything as it really is.

I always thought that there was an 'Aha!' moment when this realisation comes. But you are saying that it is a gradual process.

It is a gradual process but when you finally get it, it is sudden – 'Oh! I am That.' You are still the same thing, and appear to be the same thing as before, only before you did not know that you are That. That is with us but we don't know that it is with us, and we don't know that we are peace and bliss-absolute ourselves. When the dirt is removed, we see we are That and we have been That always.

It is just like a man who has a heavy purse in his pocket but has forgotten all about it.

He says, 'I have no money at all. I am a beggar.'

Someone comes to him and says, 'You forgot about all those coins in your pocket.'

He puts his hand in his pocket, 'Oh! I have a lot of money, I am a wealthy man!'

That is what we are doing now. We are bliss itself and we are pretending that we are miserable creatures in this world. The *guru* comes and tells us we are not miserable, we are peace and bliss-absolute; we have just forgotten. Meditate on That and you will be able to realise your own Self, which is absolute immortal peace and bliss.

Are you saying that if we have purified the mind and we are ready, when the **guru** *comes and tells us who we are, then there is this 'Aha!' moment, which is recognition of Truth?*

That's correct.

And after that moment of recognition we see clearly but there is still a deepening of the realisation?

One who has realised the Truth and his oneness with the all-pervading reality can say, 'I am bliss myself.' But there is still another state. He has not accepted the entire universe as the form of God or as his own manifestation.

When you are in the state beyond body consciousness and you are immersed in the Self, you have the most blissful experience, oblivious to external things. This is called *nirvikalpa samadhi*. When you come out of it you are once more mixing with the world. You have not accepted the world as the form of God and as the form of your own Self, so the mind is disturbed and wants to go back to that stillness. But after further spiritual practices you realise that the manifestation is your own, and it is not different from you. You can live and move in the world accepting everything as God Himself. That is *sahaja samadhi*, absorbed in natural being. When you are fully established in it you are full of peace, whether you are active or still.

So are you saying that the 'Aha!' moment is Self-realisation and full establishment in the Self is enlightenment? Are you saying that they are two different states?

You accept the entire universe as the manifestation of God and you become established in That.

You would call that enlightenment?

That is full enlightenment. Those who have realised the Truth, but have not accepted the universe as the manifestation of their own Self, as God, they still can be called *jivanmuktas* for they are liberated souls. When their ego has merged in the *paramatman* (supreme soul) or the *parabrahman* (supreme universal Truth) and there are no more rebirths, they can be called realised souls. But the fullest realisation is to accept the universe as the manifestation of God. Then they live as free, liberated souls, though apparently they are like ordinary people. You cannot find any difference in them except that they are always blissful. That is the *sahaja samadhi*.

And that is the natural state of a human being?

That is the natural state.

So there is nothing really special in this?

There is absolutely no effort for fully realised souls. Whatever they do is spontaneous. They have completely eradicated the ego, it is gone! God alone is working through them. There is no 'I' there. The small 'I' has gone completely.

And would you say that this is very rare and that there are very few people who achieve this?

Very, very rare. It is the highest attainment and very few persons are that. I know of two. I had the great privilege to live with them for some time – Ramdas and Mother Krishnabai.

Can you suggest some other people who come into this category?

It is very difficult, it is not easy to recognise them. The only way to recognise them is if many people go to them for advice, help and peace. When we go to them and sit at their feet, somehow our mind becomes still and all the waves disappear because of their influence. When someone has that experience and endless peace is dawning in them, then we can say that this is a *jivanmukta*, a realised soul, and he is in *sahaja samadhi*; he is absorbed in natural being. That is the only way we can find out.

So is it possible that there are many others that we don't know about, who are just living very simple ordinary lives and not attracting attention?

There may be, unknown to the world. But where there is a drop of honey, there are ants.

We are the ants! (laughs)

They cannot avoid it.

It appears essential to meet a **guru** *and stay with that* **guru**. *Who is the* **guru**? *What is the* **guru**'s *role? How to recognise a* **guru**?

It is essential for people on the path to get real guidance from a realised person. He is called the *guru*. But to find the *guru*, as I told you, it is not easy. We may see many people approaching him and adoring him, so we can also go there and sit at his feet in all humility. Then we will experience peace and bliss radiating from him and we can say that he is the one that can be trusted and who can guide us. I can then say I will accept him as my *guru* and serve him and love him and take guidance from him.

But we should not stay with him too long. When we stay with him too long we start finding faults. First we consider him divine, but if we stay with him for too long we start seeing faults, and then we see him only as a human being. That is not good for the spiritual aspirant. So stay with the *guru* for some time and then go away and practise independently, alone somewhere. That is more beneficial. But come to the *guru* often for guidance.

You are not suggesting going to another **guru**, *you are suggesting spending time alone?*

Staying alone, that's better. Even if you have to go to another *guru* you should look upon him as a manifestation of the same *guru*, the same Truth. The *guru* is only one, only the forms are different. The *guru* is God Himself and that is the way we should look upon him.

What tends to happen is that a devotee stays with one teacher until either the devotee sees faults in the teacher or the teacher shows the devotee something he doesn't like. Then perhaps he moves to another teacher. It happens many times. For the spiritual aspirant it is a fall, and he has to get up from it. It will take some time, it can waste time and energy. Sometimes one lifetime is wasted.

So it is important to stay with one teacher? It is a waste of time going from teacher to teacher?

Stay with one teacher. Cling to one teacher. Do *sadhana* independently, sincerely, perfectly, as guided by him. Somebody wrote to our master Ramdas, 'I was told about you and your greatness. I took initiation from another saint ten years ago. As I find no improvement I am thinking of coming to you and requesting initiation from you.' He also added, 'I have asked my *guru* for permission to come to you.' His *guru* wrote back to him saying, 'It is all right for you to go and get initiation from Swami Ramdas if it is going to help you. But one thing, if you had followed the instructions I gave you at the time of your initiation you would have felt no need to go anywhere else.'

So Swami Ramdas wrote back to him, 'Your *guru* has said correctly that if you had followed his teachings perfectly you would not find the need to go in the search of another. Even if you take initiation from Swami Ramdas and do not follow the instructions, nothing is going to happen and you are not going to benefit in any way.'

So what is required on the part of the spiritual aspirant is to sincerely follow the instructions of the *guru*, and intense *sadhana* is essential. Without that, nothing can be gained.

So what you are saying is that whatever the practice, devotion to the **guru** *is needed?*

Devotion is needed.

And you are saying that it is important for the devotee to find the right **guru**?

Yes.

It has been said that when the student is ready, the master appears. Is that your experience?

That's right.

So it is not really necessary to search for a teacher?

You may be seeking a teacher, but when you pray sincerely to God, 'Oh! God guide me to a teacher who will give me directions so that I may reach You,' then it is God's responsibility either to bring the *guru* to the disciple or bring the disciple to the *guru*. Somehow you meet up, you accept him as your *guru* and your spiritual practice begins. God arranges everything if we are sincere.

By sincere, you mean a single-pointed desire for liberation?

That's right. When we are groping in darkness we don't know how to open the door because it is so dark. So we pray.

Sri Ramana's devotees had tremendous devotion to him and he to Arunachala. Please say something about **bhakti,** *devotion, in the pursuit of awakening.*

If the devotees are sincere, if they are one hundred percent devoted to the *guru*, they must look upon the *guru* as God Himself. They must serve him, think about him day and night, and dedicate their life to him. Naturally the *guru* also watches over all of the devotees, this comes automatically.

On the devotional path, the path of *bhakti*, the devotees praise the *guru*. Sometimes a devotee comes to him and asks, 'What service can I do for you?' The *guru* doesn't need any service, he says, 'Do your *sadhana* properly, think of God constantly, that itself is sufficient to make me happy.' That is what the *guru* really wants, he does not want any other service.

What does the **guru** *want from the disciple?*

The *guru* wants him to find true devotion to God. When I am devoted to God I think of God always, I love everybody and I serve everybody as well as possible. Only then will the *guru* be pleased. To say, 'I am devoted to God, but I don't like my neighbour, I don't like my brother,' that is not devotion. A real devotee loves everybody.

Because he sees God in everybody?

Yes. And not just in everybody but in every creature.

Is there a danger that the devotee will become too attached to the form of the teacher?

That is also a danger but from the very beginning the *guru* hammers it into the disciple that he should be looked upon not as the body but as the Self. They always say don't get attached to this body, this body will perish one day or another and then you will feel bad about it. But be attached to the Truth within this body, cling to the Truth and not this body.

*In spite of all this, some devotees become attached to the **guru's** form and naturally they feel the separation when the **guru** drops the body. When Sri Ramana was about to leave his body his disciples were very upset and begging him, 'Don't leave, don't leave.' He said, 'Where could I go…'*

'… I am here only; I am in your own heart.'

So the true devotee will understand this, and it will be his experience?

Right.

Seekers often have curious ideas about the enlightened state. Can you tell us how the enlightened one sees and acts in the world?

I cannot say that they see nothing in the world. They see the world, they see the names and forms, and they know that they are all the forms of God. God Himself has taken different forms and God Himself is playing this eternal drama. That is their vision. They are conscious of the physical part of the universe as well as the spiritual substratum, they are conscious of both.

They are always in bliss but emotions are still coming and going?

They are established in their own Self, but when they see something wrong then they feel bad about it, when they see something good then they will be happy about it. This is part of their nature and they are witnesses of what is happening in this nature. They don't identify themselves with the universe or with the nature, but they remain as witnesses. At the same time, when bad things happen they will feel sorrow.

For example, Papa Ramdas might say, 'Ramdas is sorry to hear about the passing of your father.' I would ask him, 'Why do you feel sorry when you know the Truth that everything passes?' 'Oh, even sorrow is all right, it belongs to nature, it is part of the play, and it is all false.' So these expressions of different feelings are also possible in realised souls, but at the same time they remain perfectly safe in their own Self, always peaceful and blissful.

Can they be angry also?

They can be angry. But their anger is righteous indignation. It is harmless and it is only to set others right. When Mother was seriously ill, before she passed away, they would ask her, 'Mother, how are you?' She would say, 'The body is suffering a lot but I am perfectly peaceful and happy.' The realised soul knows they are not the body. Ignorant people only have the body, nothing more than that.

You have given us a profound discourse on awakening. When you meet someone with a passion for awakening, what would your short advice be?

We have to tell him that he has to work for enlightenment, he has to purify his mind and pass through a course of *sadhana* prescribed for him for that purpose. He should take the advice of some saint, get initiation, then he will be able to get enlightenment. This is how I would guide him.

When you say initiation, do you mean become a **sannyasin** *(renunciate)?*

Not necessary. Initiation is when a disciple goes before a saint and asks for spiritual help. The saint gives him a particular name of God to repeat always, for the purification of his mind. To become a *sannyasin* is also an initiation but this is at a later stage. If he has purified his mind to a certain extent he is initiated into an order of *sannyas*, if he is fit for it.

Before you go I would like to read you one paragraph from Master (Ramdas) about what a saint is:

> A saint is he who has attained the eternal, lives in the eternal and has realised the eternal. Call the great reality by any name, the eternal, God or Truth. Such a saint is a veritable blessing upon this earth. By his contact thousands are saved from the clutches of doubt, sorrow and death. He lives what he preaches and preaches what he lives. He exerts a wonderful influence and creates in the hearts of ignorant men a consciousness of their inherent divinity. He awakens the sleeping soul into the awareness of their immortal soul and all-blissful nature. By his very presence he lifts the hearts of people out of their brazen and unbridled passions. The faithful derive the greatest benefit by communion with him.

I think that you have amply done that tonight. Thank you, it has been very beautiful to talk with you. It is all very clear and very heartful. Thank you.

Om Sri Ram Jay Ram, Jay, Jay, Ram.

Who Am I?
Nan Yar

Nan Yar – Who Am I? is the standard introduction to the teachings of Bhagavan Sri Ramana Maharshi. Originally, these answers were written by Sri Ramana in the sand of Arunachala in 1901, when he would have been twenty-one years old. They were given in response to questions asked by Sivaprakasam Pillai. The original work was rewritten in the 1920s by Sri Ramana and is one of the few texts edited and approved by him.

Notes for the Reader

Sri Ramana Maharshi's original text is printed here exactly as he edited it in the 1920s. Where there is a Sanskrit word in the text we have given its meaning, italicised in square brackets. A Glossary entry for a Sanskrit word is marked in the text by a star*. Where the original translated English is old fashioned a modern word is offered, italicised in square brackets.

The curved brackets are from the original text. In the case of some answers, for example question 1, we offer a simple modern essence of the Indian terminology under the original in italicised square brackets. In these ways we intend this important text to be more available to the contemporary general reader.

All living beings desire to be happy always, without any misery. In everyone there is observed supreme love for oneself. And happiness alone is the cause of love. In order therefore, to gain that happiness which is one's nature and which is experienced in the state of deep sleep, where there is no mind, one should know oneself. To achieve this, the Path of Knowledge, the inquiry in the form of 'Who am I?', is the principal means.

1. Who am I?

The gross [*physical*] body which is composed of the seven humours (*dhatus*) [*body tissues*], I am not; the five cognitive sense organs, such as the senses of hearing, touch, sight, taste and smell, which apprehend their respective objects, namely sound, touch, colour, taste and odour, I am not; the five cognitive sense organs, such as the organs of speech, locomotion, grasping, excreting and enjoying, I am not; the five vital airs, such as prana [*life force*], which perform respectively the five functions of in-breathing, I am not; even the mind which thinks, I am not; the nescience [*ignorance*] too, which is endowed only with the residual impressions of objects and in which there are no objects and no functions, I am not.

[*I am not the physical body, nor the five senses, nor the thinking mind. I am not the unconscious mind containing the tendencies of mind, which remain even in deep sleep.*]

2. If I am none of these, then who am I?

After negating all of the above mentioned as 'not this', 'not this', this Awareness which alone remains – that I am.

3. What is the nature of Awareness?

The nature of Awareness is Existence [*Being*]-Consciousness-Bliss.

4. When will the realisation of the Self be gained?

When the world which is what-is-seen has been removed, there will be realisation of the Self which is the Seer.

[*When the perception of the world is not taken as real, there will be realisation of the Self, which is the one who sees.*]

5. Will there not be realisation of the Self even while the world is there (taken as real)?
There will not be.

6. Why?
The seer and the object seen are like the rope and the snake. Just as the knowledge of the rope which is the substratum [*essence*] will not arise unless the false knowledge of the illusory serpent goes, so the realisation of the Self which is the substratum will not be gained unless the belief that the world is real is removed.

7. When will the world which is the object seen be removed?
When the mind, which is the cause of all cognition [*knowledge*] and of all actions, becomes quiescent [*still*], the world will disappear.

8. What is the nature of the mind?
What is called 'mind' is a wondrous power residing in the Self. It causes all thoughts to arise. Apart from thoughts, there is no such thing as mind. Therefore, thought is the nature of mind. Apart from thoughts, there is no independent entity called the world. In deep sleep there are no thoughts, and there is no world. In the states of waking and dream, there are thoughts, and there is a world also. Just as the spider emits the thread (of the web) out of itself and again withdraws it into itself, likewise the mind projects the world out of itself and again resolves it into itself. When the mind comes out of the Self, the world appears. Therefore, when the world appears (to be real), the Self does not appear; and when the Self appears (shines) the world does not appear [*is not taken as real*]. When one persistently inquires into the nature of the mind, the mind will end leaving the Self (as the residue). What is referred to as the Self is the Atman*. The mind always exists only in dependence on something gross [*physical*]; it cannot stay alone. It is the mind [*ego*] that is called the subtle body or the soul (*jiva**).

9. What is the path of inquiry for understanding the nature of the mind?
That which rises as 'I' in this body is the mind. If one inquires as to

where in the body the thought 'I' rises first, one would discover that it rises in the Heart [hridayam*, *spiritual heart*]. That is the place of the mind's origin. Even if one thinks constantly 'I-I', one will be led to that place. Of all the thoughts that arise in the mind, the 'I'- thought is the first. It is only after the rise of this that the other thoughts arise. It is after the appearance of the first personal pronoun [*I*] that the second and the third personal pronouns [*you, he, she and they*] appear; without the first personal pronoun there will not be the second and the third.

10. How will the mind become quiescent [still]?
By the inquiry 'Who am I?' The thought 'Who am I?' will destroy all other thoughts, and like the stick used for stirring the burning pyre [*funeral fire*], it will itself in the end get destroyed. Then, there will arise Self-realisation.

11. What is the means for constantly holding on to the thought 'Who am I?'
When other thoughts arise, one should not pursue them, but should inquire: 'To whom do they arise?' It does not matter how many thoughts arise. As each thought arises, one should inquire with diligence [*constant effort*], 'To whom has this thought arisen?' The answer that would emerge would be 'to me'. Thereupon if one inquires 'Who am I?', the mind will go back to its source; and the thought that arose will become quiescent [*still*]. With repeated practice in this manner, the mind will develop the skill to stay in its source.

When the mind that is subtle goes out through the brain and the sense-organs, the gross [*physical*] names and forms appear; when it stays in the heart, the names and forms disappear. Not letting the mind go out, but retaining it in the Heart is what is called 'inwardness' (*antarmukha*). Letting the mind go out of the Heart is known as 'externalisation' (*bahirmukha*).

When the mind stays in the Heart, the 'I', which is the source of all thoughts will go, and the Self which ever exists will shine. Whatever one does, one should do without the egoity 'I'. If one acts in that way, all will appear as of the nature of *Shiva** (God).

12. Are there no other means for making the mind quiescent [still]?
Other than inquiry, there are no adequate means. If through other means it is sought to control the mind, the mind will appear to be controlled, but will again go forth [*arise*]. Through the control of breath also, the mind will become quiescent; but it will be quiescent only so long as the breath remains controlled, and when the breath resumes the mind also will again start moving and will wander as impelled [*driven*] by residual impressions [*thoughts*]. The source is the same for both mind and breath. Thought, indeed, is the nature of the mind.

The thought 'I' is the first thought of the mind; and that is egoity. It is from that whence egoity originates that breath also originates. Therefore, when the mind becomes quiescent, the breath is controlled, and when the breath is controlled the mind becomes quiescent. But in deep sleep, although the mind becomes quiescent, the breath does not stop.

This is because of the will of God, so that the body may be preserved and other people may not be under the impression that it is dead. In the state of waking and in *samadhi** [*glimpse of the Self*], when the mind becomes quiescent the breath is controlled. Breath is the gross [*physical*] form of the mind. Till the time of death, the mind keeps breath in the body; and when the body dies, the mind takes the breath along with it. Therefore, the exercise of breath control is only an aid for rendering the mind quiescent (*manonigraha*); it will not destroy the mind (*manonasa**). Like the practice of breath control, meditation on the forms of God, repetition of *mantras** [*sacred sounds*], restriction on food, are but aids for rendering the mind quiescent.

Through meditation on the forms of God and through repetition of *mantras*, the mind becomes one-pointed. The mind will always be wandering. Just as when a chain is given to an elephant to hold in its trunk it will go along grasping the chain and nothing else, so also when the mind is occupied with a name or form it will grasp that alone.

When the mind expands in the form of countless thoughts, each thought becomes weak; but as thoughts get resolved the mind becomes one-pointed and strong; for such a mind Self-inquiry will become easy. Of all the restrictive rules, that relating to the taking of *sattvic** [*pure*] food in moderate quantities is the best; by observing this rule, the *sattvic* quality of mind will increase, and that will be helpful to Self-inquiry.

13. The residual impressions (thoughts) of objects appear unending like the waves of an ocean. When will all of them get destroyed?
As the meditation on the Self rises higher and higher, the thoughts will get destroyed.

14. Is it possible for the residual impressions of objects that come from beginningless time, as it were, to be resolved, and for one to remain as the pure Self?
Without yielding to the doubt 'Is it possible, or not?' one should persistently hold on to the meditation on the Self. Even if one be a great sinner, one should not worry and weep 'O! I am a sinner, how can I be saved?' One should completely renounce the thought 'I am a sinner' and concentrate keenly on mediation on the Self alone; then, one would surely succeed. There are not two minds – one good and the other evil; the mind is only one. It is the residual impressions [*thoughts*] that are of two kinds – auspicious and inauspicious. When the mind is under the influence of auspicious impressions it is called good; and when it is under the influence of inauspicious impressions it is regarded as evil.

The mind should not be allowed to wander towards worldly objects and what concerns other people. However bad other people may be, one should bear no hatred for them. Both desire and hatred should be eschewed [*avoided*].

All that one gives to others one gives to one's self. If this truth is understood who will not give to others? When one's self arises all arises; when one's self becomes quiescent [*still*] all becomes quiescent. To the extent we behave with humility, to that extent there will result good. If the mind is rendered quiescent, one may live anywhere.

15. How long should inquiry be practised?

As long as there are impressions of objects in the mind, so long the inquiry 'Who am I?' is required. As thoughts arise they should be destroyed then and there in the very place of their origin, through inquiry. If one resorts to contemplation of the Self unintermittently [*constantly*], until the Self is gained, that alone would do. As long as there are enemies within the fortress, they will continue to sally forth [*come out*]; if they are destroyed as they emerge, the fortress will fall into our hands.

16. What is the nature of the Self?

What exists is the Self alone. The world, the individual soul and God are appearances in it, like silver in mother-of-pearl; these three appear at the same time and disappear at the same time. The Self is that where there is absolutely no 'I'-thought. That is called 'Silence'. The Self itself is the world; the Self itself is 'I'; the Self itself is God; all is *Shiva*, the Self.

17. Is not everything the work of God?

Without desire, resolve, or effort, the sun rises; and in its mere presence, the sun-stone emits fire, the lotus blooms, water evaporates, people perform their various functions and then rest. Just as in the presence of the magnet the needle moves, it is by virtue of the mere presence of God that the souls governed by the three (cosmic) functions [*creation, sustaining life and dissolution*] or the fivefold divine activity [Vedantic *theory of creation*] perform their actions and then rest, in accordance with their respective *karmas** [*cosmic law*].

God has no resolve [*intention*]; no *karma* attaches itself to Him. That is like worldly actions not affecting the sun, or like the merits and demerits [*good and bad qualities*] of the other four elements not affecting all-pervading space.

18. Of the devotees, who is the greatest?

He who gives himself up to the Self that is God is the most excellent devotee. Giving one's self up to God means remaining constantly in the Self without giving room for the rise of any thoughts other than that of the Self.

Whatever burdens are thrown on God, He bears them. Since the supreme power of God makes all things move, why should we, without submitting ourselves to it, constantly worry ourselves with thoughts as to what should be done and how, and what should not be done and how not? We know that the train carries all loads, so after getting on it why should we carry our small luggage on our head to our discomfort, instead of putting it down in the train and feeling at ease?

19. What is non-attachment?

As thoughts arise, destroying them utterly without any residue in the very place of their origin is non-attachment. Just as the pearl-diver ties a stone to his waist, sinks to the bottom of the sea and there takes the pearls, so each one of us should be endowed with non-attachment, dive within oneself and obtain the Self-Pearl.

20. Is it possible for God and the Guru to effect the liberation of a soul?

God and the *Guru* will only show the way to liberation; they will not by themselves take the soul to the state of liberation. In truth, God and the *Guru* are not different.

Just as the prey which has fallen into the jaws of a tiger has no escape, so those who have come within the ambit [*presence*] of the *Guru's* gracious look will be saved by the *Guru* and will not get lost; yet, each one should, by his own effort pursue the path shown by God or *Guru* and gain liberation.

One can know oneself only with one's own eye of knowledge, and not with somebody else's. Does he who is Rama require the help of a mirror to know that he is Rama?

21. Is it necessary for one who longs for liberation to inquire into the nature of categories (tattvas) [Vedantic system categorising existence]?

Just as one who wants to throw away garbage has no need to analyse it and see what it is, so one who wants to know the Self has no need to count the number of categories or inquire into their characteristics;

what he has to do is to reject altogether the categories that hide the Self. The world should be considered like a dream.

22. Is there no difference between waking and dream?
Waking is long and dream short; other than this there is no difference. Just as waking happenings seem real while awake, so do those in a dream while dreaming. In dream the mind takes on another body. In both waking and dream states thoughts, names and forms occur simultaneously.

23. Is it any use reading books for those who long for liberation?
All the texts say that in order to gain liberation one should render the mind quiescent [*still*]; therefore their conclusive teaching is that the mind should be rendered quiescent; once this has been understood there is no need for endless reading.

In order to quieten the mind one has only to inquire within oneself what one's Self is; how could this search be done in books? One should know one's Self with one's own eye of wisdom. The Self is within the five sheaths [*body, breath, mind, intellect, ignorance*]; but books are outside them. Since the Self has to be inquired into by discarding the five sheaths, it is futile to search for it in books. There will come a time when one will have to forget all that one has learned.

24. What is happiness?
Happiness is the very nature of the Self; happiness and the Self are not different. There is no happiness in any object of the world. We imagine through our ignorance that we derive happiness from objects. When the mind goes out, it experiences misery. In truth, when its desires are fulfilled, it returns to its own place and enjoys the happiness that is the Self. Similarly, in the states of sleep, *samadhi* and fainting, and when the object desired is obtained or the object disliked is removed, the mind becomes inward-turned, and enjoys pure Self-Happiness.

Thus the mind moves without rest alternately going out of the Self and returning to it. Under the tree the shade is pleasant; out in the open the heat is scorching. A person who has been going about in the sun feels cool when he reaches the shade. Someone who keeps on going from the shade into the sun and then back into the shade is a fool. A wise man stays permanently in the shade.

Similarly, the mind of the one who knows the truth does not leave *Brahman* [absolute reality]*. The mind of the ignorant, on the contrary, revolves in the world, feeling miserable, and for a little time returns to *Brahman* to experience happiness. In fact, what is called the world is only thought. When the world disappears, i.e., when there is no thought, the mind experiences happiness; and when the world appears, it goes through misery.

25. *What is wisdom-insight* (jnana drishti)?
Remaining quiet is what is called wisdom-insight. To remain quiet is to resolve the mind in the Self. Telepathy, knowing past, present and future happenings and clairvoyance do not constitute wisdom-insight.

26. *What is the relation between desirelessness and wisdom?*
Desirelessness is wisdom. The two are not different; they are the same. Desirelessness is refraining from turning the mind towards any objects. Wisdom means the appearance of no object. In other words, not seeking what is other than the Self is detachment or desirelessness; not leaving the Self is wisdom.

27. *What is the difference between inquiry and meditation?*
Inquiry consists in retaining [*keeping*] the mind in the Self. Meditation consists in thinking that one's self is *Brahman*, Existence [*Being*]-Consciousness-Bliss.

28. *What is liberation?*
Inquiring into the nature of one's self that is in bondage, and realising one's true nature is liberation.

Glossary

Advaita — Non-duality; a school of *Vedanta* philosophy teaching the Oneness of God, soul, and universe, whose chief exponent was *Adi Shankara*.

ahamkara — The ego that considers itself as an 'acting I'.

ajna — Third eye *chakra*. Located between the eyebrows. Intuition and wisdom.

ajnani — One who has not realised the Self; unenlightened.

anahata — (Lit: unstruck sound) Heart *chakra*. Located in the centre of the chest. Unconditional love, compassion and neutrality.

ananda — Bliss. One of the three qualities of the Self: *sat-chit-ananda*.

Arjuna — Main male figure from the *Bhagavad Gita* who receives instruction from Lord *Krishna* about the nature of being and the meaning of life. *Arjuna* represents the human being caught in ignorance.

artha — One of the four 'goals of life'. Considered to be a noble goal as long as it follows the dictates of *Vedic* morality. The concept includes achieving widespread fame, garnering wealth and having an elevated social standing.

artharthi — One who desires material gain (*artha*).

Arunachala — Holy mountain at Tiruvannamalai in South India. Considered to be *Shiva*. Sri Ramana Maharshi called *Arunachala* his *guru*. He arrived there aged sixteen and never left.

Arunachaleswara — Hindu temple dedicated to Lord *Shiva*, located at the foot of *Arunachala*, Tiruvannamalai; home of Lord *Shiva* and his wife Parvati. The inner sanctum is more than two thousand years old.

ashram — In ancient India a Hindu hermitage where sages lived in peace and tranquility amidst nature. Today, the term *ashram* is usually used to refer to an intentional community formed primarily for spiritual upliftment of its members, often headed by a religious leader or mystic.

atman	The inmost Self or Spirit of man.
avatar	Incarnation (becoming flesh) of a god, the Divine. The term *avatar* has many similarities with the term 'messiah' in other religions.
Bhagavad Gita	A portion of the *Mahabharata* in which Lord *Krishna*, an incarnation of Lord *Vishnu*, gives spiritual instructions to *Arjuna*.
Bhagavan	God. Respectful title for a realised being.
Bhagavatam	Classical Indian text describing the life of Lord *Shiva*.
bhajan	(Lit: to worship) Song with religious content, which is often dedicated to specific gods.
bhakta	Devotee.
bhakti	Devotion, love. Traditionally, one of the principal approaches to God-realisation.
bhakti marga	The path of devotion.
bhavana	Development, cultivation.
Bodhisattva	One who has gained complete liberation; an enlightened being who is no longer caught in the cycle of birth and death, yet continues to incarnate out of compassion until all sentient beings are awakened.
Brahma	The creator. With *Shiva* (the destroyer) and *Vishnu* (the preserver), one of the main Hindu deities.
brahma bhava	Being in *Brahman*.
Brahman	The impersonal, absolute reality – the Self.
Brahma Sutra	Also known as *Vedanta Sutra*; cryptic statements whose subject matter is *Brahman*.
Buddha	Usually refers to *Gautama Buddha*, the founder of Buddhism, often referred to simply as 'the *Buddha*'. A *buddha* (Sanskrit: awakened) is any being who has become fully awakened.
buddhi	A feminine *Sanskrit* noun derived from the root *budh* – to be awake, to understand, to know.
Chaitanya	Consciousness; or *Chaitanya Mahaprabhu*: a 16th century Hindu saint, well-known for his devotion to Lord *Krishna*.

Glossary

chakra	(Lit: wheel) One of the seven subtle energy centres in the body, located on a line from the perineum to the crown of the head.
Deepam	One of the oldest festivals of light celebrated by Tamil Hindus on the full moon day of the month of Karthikai (Nov/Dec). Houses and streets are lit up with rows of oil lamps. The huge lamp is lit on the peak of the holy mountain, *Arunachala*, Tiruvannamalai.
dharma	Practice or path of Truth.
dhyana/dhyanam	(Lit: meditation) The state of deep meditation. Equivalent term is 'Zen' in Buddhism.
drisha	The world of objects.
dukha	Sorrow.
gunas	The three qualities of all manifestation: *sattva* (purity), *rajas* (activity) and *tamas* (sluggishness).
guru	A teacher in the religious or spiritual sense, commonly used in Hinduism, Buddhism, and Sikhism. The *guru* is seen in these religions as a sacred conduit for wisdom and guidance. In many branches of the aforementioned religions, the importance of finding a true *guru* is given as a prerequisite for attaining Self-realisation.
Iswara	The Lord; the Almighty.
japam	Practice of repetition of the Lord's name or of a *mantra*.
jiva	(Lit: living being) The individual soul, which, until liberation, will continue to incarnate. In essence, it is one with the Universal Soul.
jivanmukta	One who is liberated while still alive.
jivatman	The individual aspect of atman; the 'opposite pole' is *paramatman*, the absolute aspect of *atman*.
jnana	Knowledge of what is real and what is not real. A principal, traditional path to realisation of the final Reality, the Self.
jnana marga	The path of knowledge.
Jnana Vasishta	Teachings of the master and saint *Vasishta*, who is considered the incarnation of *Brahma*; and the title of the book in which this teaching is explained.

jnani	One who has realised the Self. One who has attained realisation by the path of knowledge, meaning the knowledge of what is real and what is not real.
kamana	Desire, wish.
karma	(Lit: action) Cosmic law of cause and effect, the result of an individual's past action, which is said to invariably return to him at some point in time. Also: the collective storehouse of merit or demerit from all of an individual's past actions.
karma yoga	The *yoga* of action based on the teachings of the *Bhagavad Gita*. Focuses on the adherence to duty while remaining detached from the reward. It states that one can attain salvation (*moksha*) or love of God (*bhakti*) by performing one's duties in an unselfish manner.
kashaya	Hidden desires.
Kenopanishad	One of the older, primary *Upanishads* commented upon by *Shankara*.
Krishna	(Lit: all-attractive) Incarnation of *Vishnu*, who is considered the Supreme God. Usually depicted as a young cowherd playing a flute or as a youthful prince giving philosophical instruction. Represents knowledge and bliss.
leela	The play of God; divine play.
lingam	A symbol of the Divine, in the form of a phallus, for the Hindu god, *Shiva*.
Mahabharata	Great epic of the Bharata people. National epic of India. Consists of 106,000 couplets. Existed in various forms for well over two thousand years. It's most famous text is the *Bhagavad Gita*.
mahatma	(Lit: great soul) Great man or saint.
mala	(Lit: bead) *Japa mala* is a circle of 108 beads, like a rosary, often used as an aid for repetition of a *mantra*.
mananam	Reflection; the second of the three main methods to reach *jnana*.
manipura	(Lit: city of jewels) Navel *chakra*. Located just above the navel. Life force, will and transformation.
manokara	Thinking mind.

Glossary

manolaya	Absorbed state of the mind, which is temporal in nature.
manonasa	Literally: extinction of the mind. It particularly means destruction of the thinking mind as the practical mind is needed for daily functioning.
mantra	Sacred sound. In the Hindu traditions a sound from the *Vedas*. Repeated either orally or mentally and used as an aid in bringing concentration to the mind. The most well-known *mantra* is the original sound *om*.
manushyatvam	Humanity. Assemblage of all specific qualities that distinguish man from other beings, including those higher values which are essentially human.
marga	A path.
maya	Worldly illusion, mistaking the transient for the real; non-awareness of actuality, appearances masquerading as reality.
mithya	(Lit: unreal) In Hindu thought, the world as we see it is unreal, and is only a projection of God.
moksha	Liberation from *samsara*, the cycle of death and rebirth and all of the suffering and limitations of worldly existence.
mukti	Release. See *moksha*.
muladhara	Base or root *chakra*. Located in the region between the genitals and the anus. Grounding, instinct and survival.
mumukshu	One who desires liberation.
mumukshutvam	The desire to achieve liberation.
nididhyasanam	Final step of the three-step process towards Self-realisation; involves deep meditation and requires *mumukshutvam*.
nitya	Forever, eternal, beyond the influence of time.
nirvana	Blowing out, such as a flame. Annihilation of desire, passion and ego; liberation, characterised by freedom and bliss.
om	Cosmic, eternal sound.
omkara	Same as the sacred, mystical syllable *om*.
papa	Sin, crime, evil; negative consequences of bad acts.

parabrahman	The Supreme *Brahman*.
paramatman	Highest, divine *atman*. *Atman* is the Higher Self of human beings; *paramatman* is the Higher Self of God.
Periya Purana	One of the Hindu scriptures speaking about *Shiva*.
prakasha	Radiating beam, clarity, light. Also the ability to see reality clearly.
prakriti	Essential nature, eternal power.
Prakriya	A category of the *Upanishads* that deals with different teaching methods.
pranayama	Breath control.
prarabdha	(Lit: begun, undertaken) One of the three types of *karma*. The fruit of all of our past actions that now has its effect. Destiny or fate.
prasad	A gift of food from the *guru*, usually handed out at the end of *Satsang*, though often also distributed on religious occasions at temples and shrines.
prem	Love.
premananda	Unconditional love and bliss.
puja	Worship. Ritual in which offerings are made and prayers said.
punya	Good *karma* created by good thoughts, words and actions. Generated by giving, kindness and *dharma* practice.
purna	Completeness, fullness.
purusharta	Human effort, individual exertion, ideal.
rajas	One of the three *gunas*. Quality of activity, passion, birth, creativity. The fruit is often pain, even though the immediate effect is pleasure.
reiki	Japanese form of healing using the life force energy by laying hands above the body.
sadguru/satguru	The *guru* who leads one to freedom – Self-realisation.
sadhaka	Spiritual seeker.
sadhana	Spiritual practice.

Glossary

sadhu	(Lit: right, holy) A pious or righteous man. Traditionally a renunciate, a wanderer with a bare minimum of possessions, who relies on alms for daily needs.
sahaja samadhi	Highest state of enlightenment. Effortless and permanent.
sahasrara	(Lit: thousand-petaled lotus) Crown *chakra*. Located at the top of the head. Ultimate Self-knowing and understanding.
sakshat sadhana	*Sadhana* of the direct path of God-realisation.
samadhi	A non-dualistic state of consciousness. The experiencing subject becomes one with the experienced object, the mind becomes still. Direct but temporary experience of the Self.
samsara	The continuous cycle of birth and death caused by illusion and desire.
sangha	The community or gathering of devotees around a *guru*.
sannyasin	Renunciate, who, after being initiated by a *guru* or religious superior, is given a spiritual name and takes vows to abandon all ties with conventional society and live with one-pointed attention on God only.
Sanskrit	(Lit: refined, consecrated, sanctified) Ancient language of the *Vedas*. In Hinduism and Buddhism it was regarded as 'the language of the gods'. Nowadays used mainly for religious and scientific discourse. Origin of all Indo-Germanic languages.
sastra	Sacred scriptures.
sat	Truth.
satchitananda	Truth – consciousness – bliss. The three qualities of the Absolute, *Brahman*.
satchitananda brahma	'*Brahman* is Truth, consciousness and bliss.'
satori	(Japanese: enlightenment) Awakening to the profound understanding of the true nature of existence.
Satsang	(Lit: abiding in the Truth) The gathering of the *guru* with his students.
sattva	Purity, goodness; the highest of the three *gunas*.

169

sattvic	Pure. Anglicised adjective from *sattva*.
sattvika	One who is endowed with goodness, one who is pure and still.
satya	Truth.
Self	The term most commonly used in translation for *Atman*; the unchanging awareness, consciousness itself.
shakti	The power of becoming, the energy of creation; as goddess, the female aspect of *Shiva*.
Shankara	*Adi Shankara*: Indian sage of the 9th century who is considered the most influential figure of *Advaita Vedanta*.
shishya	A pupil or disciple, especially one who has proven himself and has formally been accepted by a *guru*.
Shiva	The destroyer. With *Brahma* (the creator) and *Vishnu* (the preserver), one of the main Hindu deities.
shraddha	Faith and trust.
shradda shastra	Trust in the *Vedic* scriptures; especially that these texts contain higher knowledge which reveals the timeless, 'seen' Truth. In the wider sense: trust in God.
shravanam	Listening, hearing.
siddha	A person who has achieved a *siddhi*.
siddhi	Supernatural power, paranormal ability.
sloka	A *Sanskrit* verse.
stitha pragna	Person of steady wisdom.
svadhisthana	Belly or sacral *chakra*. Located in the lower abdomen, centered between the navel and the genitals. Life energy, creativity and sexuality.
Swami	Title for religious attainment and scholarship.
swaroopa ananda	The highest state of bliss.
tamas	Sluggishness, inactivity, darkness. One of the three *gunas*
tantra	Asian body of beliefs and practices that works from the principle that the universe we experience is nothing other than the concrete manifestation of the divine energy. It seeks to ritually appropriate and channel that energy within the human microcosm, in creative and emancipatory ways.

Glossary

turiya	State of pure consciousness similar to *samadhi*.
Upanishad	The concluding portion of the *Vedas* consisting of 108 verses. The *Upanishads* are the texts from which all *Vedanta* philosophy is derived.
Upanishadic rishis	(Lit: *rishi* – seer) Mythological figures who channelled the *Upanishads*.
upasana	(Lit: sitting near) The way or path through which one worships the Divine.
vairagya	Dispassion, detachment, or renunciation from the pains and pleasures in the material world.
vasanas	Emotional and mental tendencies; habits of action, reaction, and desires of the persona or conditional being, which are said to be the product of patterns of living in both this life and past lives.
vasthu	Nature, a surrounding or environment.
Vedanta	A metaphysical philosophy derived from the *Upanishads*.
Vedanta sastra	*Vedic* scriptures.
Vedas	(Lit: knowledge) Four collections of scriptures that were channelled by the *rishis*. The ultimate source of authority for Hindus.
vichara	Search, investigation.
videhamukta	One liberated at the fall of the physical body.
Vishnu	One of the principal Hindu deities worshipped as the protector and preserver of the world.
Vitobha	Representative of Lord *Krishna* and *Vishnu*.
viveka	Discrimination between the permanent and the impermanent.
vrittis	Waves of mental activity.
yoga	(Lit: union) Teaching and practice derived from the ancient *Vedic* philosophy.
yoga sastra	*Yogic* scriptures.
yogi	One who practises *yoga*.

Contact Details

Author's Contact Details

John David
Open Sky House
Rheinstr. 54, 51371 Hitdorf, Germany
Phone: +49 2173 4099204
E-mail: office@meetingjohndavid.org
Website: www.meetingjohndavid.org

Masters' Contact Details

Sri Hans Raj Maharaj †
Sacha Dham Ashram
Tapovan Sarai PO
Laxman Jhula, Rishikesh 249192
Tehri Garhwal UT
Phone: +91 135 2433184
E-mail: omguru2001@yahoo.com

Ajja (Puttur Ajja) †
Ananda Kuteera
Village & PO Chikkamudnoor
Kemmai, Puttur 574203 DK Dist.
Karnataka
Phone: +91 8251 237655
E-mail: info@ajja.org.in
Website: www.myajja.org

Ramesh Balsekar †
Apartment No. 10 Sindhuli Building
Nawroji Gamadia Road, Off Peddar Road
Mumbai 400 028
Phone: +91 22 23517725
Website: www.rameshbalsekar.com

Sri Brahmam
Bhagavan Sri Ramana Maharshi Asramam
Tadipatri 515 411, Anantapur Dist.
Andrah Pradesh
Phone: +91 8558227234
E-mail: sri@brahmam.net
Website: www.brahmam.net

D. B. Gangolli †
No contact details

Radha Ma †
Gnaneshwari
Chicken Farm Road
Atiyandhal, Ramanashramam
Tiruvannamalai 606 603
Tamil Nadu
E-mail: radhagiridhar@aol.in

Swami Satchidananda †
Anandashram
Anandashram PO
Kanhangad 671 531, Kasaragod Dist.
Kerala
Phone: +91 467 2203036
E-mail: papa@anandashram.org
Website: www.anandashram.org

Sri Ramana Maharshi †
Sri Ramanasramam
Sri Ramanasramam PO
Tiruvannamalai 606 603
Tamil Nadu
Phone: +91 4175 237200
E-mail: ashram@sriramanamaharshi.org
For ordering publications:
bookstall@sriramanamaharshi.org
Website: www.sriramanamaharshi.org

ARUNACHALA PILGRIMAGE RETREAT

This Retreat is an opportunity to live in a community for three weeks at the holy mountain Arunachala in Tiruvannamalai, South India. Arunachala has been a powerful place of pilgrimage for two thousand years. We are accommodated in a lovely modern ashram. Our meetings take place on the roof directly overlooking the holy mountain. Each morning there is quiet meditation, yoga and a Meeting with John David. We spend the afternoons either alone, in Ramana Maharshi's ashram, or together with the group. Also, we go on a magical four-day bus trip that brings us to wonderful Indian Saints and allows us to see and experience Indian culture and landscapes.

www.india.meetingjohndavid.org

Open Sky House
An Experiment in Conscious Living

International Spiritual and Arts Communities

Hitdorf, Cologne, Germany
Tripillya, Kiev, Ukraine
Denia, Valencia, Spain

'At our core is a silence which never changes.
If we live from this place we are present, spontaneous, free.'

John David

The inspiration is to become still and be self-aware in our daily life. These communities are amazing and successful Experiments in Conscious Living. We are open to everybody who wants to know themselves and live consciously.

www.openskyhouse.org

Open Sky House Hitdorf
Living Together in Joyful Creativity

In 2004 the main international community began around the English spiritual teacher John David. A loving, silent energy field has developed which deeply touches many guests and volunteers who want to look inside and recognise their true nature. John David makes himself available as a guide through daily meditations, spiritual Meetings and Retreats. Daily life becomes a mirror for us to be self-aware through running the community businesses, painting, theatre, dance and music. Spoken English, German, French, Spanish and Russian.

You are welcome to visit as a Guest or a Volunteer.

www.openskyhousehitdorf.de

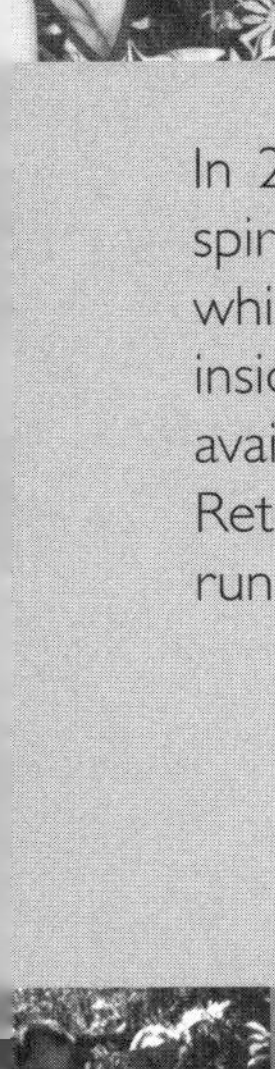

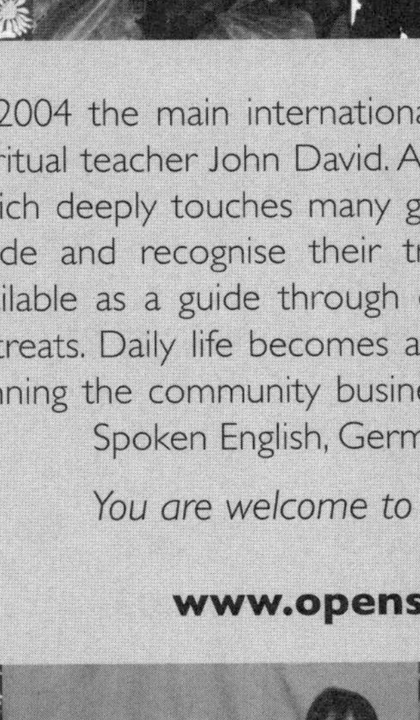

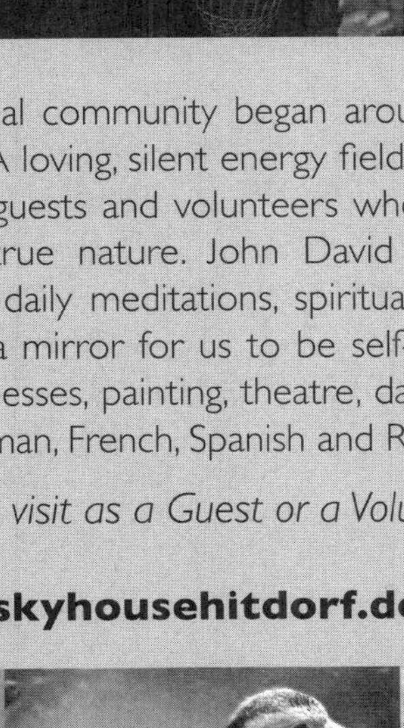

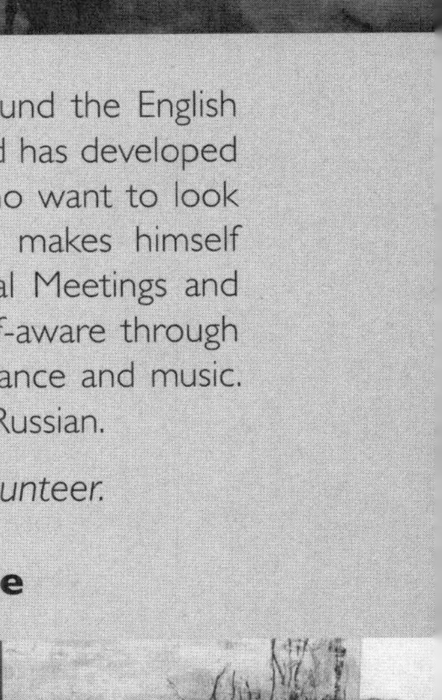

Open Sky House Tripillya
Silence in the Beauty of Nature

Since 2013 a second community has developed in Ukraine. A community house, the modern and elegant Black Cube Hotel and a lovely retreat centre are set in the wild and peaceful nature of Tripillya on the Dniepr river. Volunteers and guests are welcome to the daily life of the community, including meditations and yoga. The English spiritual teacher John David offers support and guidance on the spiritual journey by giving regular Meetings and Retreats. Beautiful nature along with the heartfulness of the Eastern Europeans creates an ambience of stillness and beauty. Spoken English and Russian.

You are welcome to visit as a Guest or a Volunteer.

www.openskyhousetripillya.com.ua

Open Sky House Denia
Celebrating every Moment

In July 2015 a third community started in Denia, near Valencia. The stunning old villa within a tropical paradise, palm trees and a large pool is only a 5 minute walk to the Mediterranean. With open doors to volunteers and guests, the invitation is to dive into the energy of silence, and to meet the English spiritual Teacher John David in Meetings and Retreats. You can take part in the daily life of the community. Be supported by daily meditation, yoga and the stillness and beauty of the area. Spoken English, Spanish, French and German.

You are welcome to visit as a Guest or a Volunteer.

www.openskyhousedenia.es

OPEN SKY PRESS
Timeless Wisdom

Nan Yar is a classic spiritual text and one of the most important books of the 20th Century. Rare words direct from one of the greatest Masters, Sri Ramana Maharshi. It offers a clear understanding of Self-enquiry and how to realise the Self. Many beautiful photos of Sri Ramana. Published in English, German, Russian and Spanish.   ISBN 978-0-9574627-5-5

The Great Misunderstanding opens our eyes to our true potential, and is for anybody who wants to find out what life is really about. It explores the transformation process of 25 people in the community, Open Sky House, with John David. The teachings in the book are supported by dialogues with the residents, and regular jokes add a playfulness and lightness. The film lays out the essence of the teachings, interweaving it with film of the community life, and John David's annual retreat in India.

The Book   ISBN 978-0-9570886-7-2
The Film   ISBN 978-0-9570886-8-9

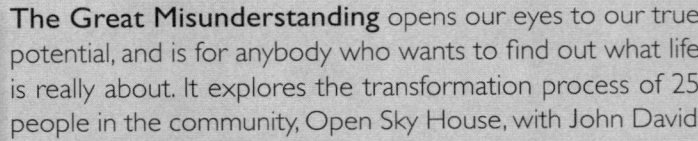

Arunachala Shiva is a profound homage to the spiritual greatness of Bhagavan Sri Ramana Maharshi, laying out his life and teachings with interviews, commentaries and beautiful color photos. The film shows the cream of the interviews in the book, along with archive material of Sri Ramana, film of the Ramana Ashram and of course, wonderful footage of Arunachala.

The Book   ISBN 978-0-9555730-6-4
The Film   ISBN 978-0-9555730-9-5

European Masters – Blueprints for Awakening is a bridge from the ancient texts and teachings of India and the East to today's modern Western life. John David interviews fourteen European spiritual Masters, some well known others little known. It's a joy to hear Non-duality explained in modern English and from a Western experience of life, giving a unique insight and a deeper exploration of freedom.

The Book   ISBN 978-0-9555730-7-1
The Film   ISBN 978-0-9566070-1-0

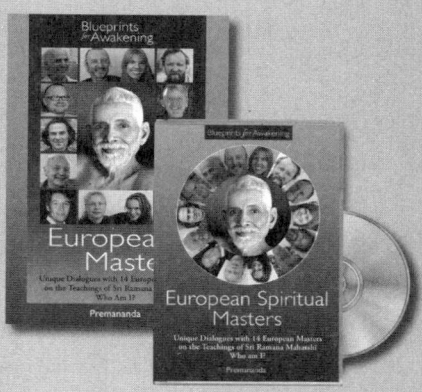

Papaji – Amazing Grace is a book of fifteen profoundly beautiful interviews with people who had an Awakening with the Advaita Master Papaji. They are stories of a housewife, a businessman, even an officer of a nuclear powered aircraft carrier. Each person, whatever their background, had the common longing to discover the eternal Truth of who they are. When this longing is strong enough a Master appears in one's life.

ISBN 978-0-9555730-0-2

Arunachala Talks consists of eight talks given spontaneously at John David's annual Arunachala Retreat in South India. John David lovingly and humorously guides us to see that we are not the experience 'my life', but rather the awareness in which the experience happens. The talks discuss the effects of devotion, trust and destiny, bringing us to presence and assisting a realisation of the truth of who we really are.

ISBN 978-0-9555730-2-6

OPEN SKY PRESS
Publishers of Fine Quality Spiritual Books

Tel +49 (0) 2173 1016070
office@openskypress.com
www.openskypress.com

Companion Films

These companion films contain the original video material from the interviews and show the energetic presence of the Masters.

Blueprints for Awakening - Wisdom of the Masters weaves together touching moments from the interviews, along with intimate meetings with the Masters, sharing their unique expression of Truth. Beautiful footage of the Masters and spiritual India.

Meeting the Master is a series of amazing films showing each Master's complete interview, with private moments from their lives. A unique archive giving a taste the Indian spiritual tradition through the grace of these Masters.

Video Website: www.blueprintsforawakening.org
Two hundred short videos of the Masters' answers to the twelve questions are available online, providing a taste of their wisdom and grace.

DVD Sampler Information

The trailer DVD includes 5 trailers of all the films published by Open Sky Press since its founding in 2007. It is a wonderful introduction to many fascinating topics, all on one disk:

- Blueprints for Awakening - Indian Masters
- European Spiritual Masters - Blueprints for Awakening
- Arunachala Shiva - Ramana Maharshi's Life and Teachings
- The Great Misunderstanding - Discover your true Happiness
- Satori - Metamorphosis of an Awakening

www.openskypress.com